IN
SEARCH
OF
COMMON
GROUND

IN
SEARCH

OF

COMMON
GROUND

Inspiring
True Stories of
Overcoming Hate
in a Divided
World

BASTIAN BERBNER

Translated by Carolin Sommer

THE EXPERIMENT

NEW YORK

IN SEARCH OF COMMON GROUND: *Inspiring True Stories of Overcoming Hate in a Divided World*
Copyright © 2019 by Verlag C.H. Beck oHG, München
Translation copyright © 2022 by Carolin Sommer

Originally published in Germany as *180 Grad: Geschichten gegen den Hass* by C. H. Beck Verlag oHG. First published in English in North America in revised form by The Experiment, LLC, in 2022.

The Experiment, LLC
220 East 23rd Street, Suite 600
New York, NY 10010-4658
theexperimentpublishing.com

THE EXPERIMENT and its colophon are registered trademarks of The Experiment, LLC. Many of the designations used by manufacturers and sellers to distinguish their products are claimed as trademarks. Where those designations appear in this book and The Experiment was aware of a trademark claim, the designations have been capitalized.

The Experiment's books are available at special discounts when purchased in bulk for premiums and sales promotions as well as for fund-raising or educational use. For details, contact us at info@theexperimentpublishing.com.

Library of Congress Cataloging-in-Publication Data available upon request

ISBN 978-1-61519-894-8
Ebook ISBN 978-1-61519-895-5

Jacket and text design by Beth Bugler
Author photograph courtesy of the author

Manufactured in the United States of America

First printing October 2022
10 9 8 7 6 5 4 3 2 1

Contents

Preface

Is there nothing we can do? That was the question that inspired this book. In the spring of 2017, I was traveling through pre-election France, a country divided. In the villages of Provence, the people protested against presidential candidate Emmanuel Macron, the "internationalist." In Paris and Lyon, the liberal elites warned against the presidential candidate Marine Le Pen, the "right-wing extremist." Those on the right acted as if Macron as president signified the end of France; those on the left prophesized fascism under Le Pen. The two camps attacked each other, not like political rivals in a scramble for power but like opponents in a fight for survival.

Across the English Channel, things were no different. British society had been split pretty much right down the middle ever since the Brexit referendum a few months earlier. Fifty-two percent of the voters had chosen to leave the European Union, which the other 48 percent considered a fatal mistake.

In the United States, the situation was even worse: The newly elected president was glorified as the savior of the American people by half the voters, but vilified by the other half as an incompetent, egotistical racist who would bring down democracy, and maybe the whole world.

For the first time, I experienced something akin to political fear. Liberal democracy and the stability of the West had become uncertain. Even a return of fascism seemed possible. Usually, fear decreases the closer we get to its cause. But here, the opposite was true: The closer I got to the crises to report on them, the greater my fear grew. As if in the grip of a virus, Western societies appeared to be splitting in two, one after the other, at an ever-increasing pace. And the process hasn't stopped.

In Italy and the Netherlands, right-wing populists are gaining in popularity. In Austria, they formed part of the government until they were brought down by a scandal involving a secret video recording in 2019. In Hungary and Poland, the populists are using their power to establish authoritarian structures. And in Germany, they first conquered the streets and then, following the migration crisis in 2015 and 2016, in one election after another, the regional parliaments.

This process could be seen as the healthy self-regulation of democracies had it not given rise to a political debate that is carried out—on both sides—with decreasing respect and humanity, and with increasing malice and hatred. The moderate, sensible, and thoughtful voices have fallen silent, and the shrill, hating, and radical ones are getting louder. Any gradations are getting lost in "either/or" and "us-against-them" arguments. A political war has broken out, and it's not just a rhetorical one.

On January 6, 2021, over two thousand right-wing supporters stormed the US Capitol in an attempt to stop the certification of the winner of the presidential election, resulting in five deaths. At a rally in Charlottesville, Virginia, in 2017, a White supremacist rams his car into a group of counter-protesters, killing a woman and injuring nineteen others. In other parts of the country, the offices of the Republican party are being attacked. At a charity event in Gdańsk, Poland, in 2019, the city's mayor, a supporter of the opposition, is stabbed to death while onstage. In Germany, refugee hostels are going up in flames, as are the cars of extreme-right politicians of the Alternative for Germany party (AfD). In Chemnitz, Nazis are again marching in the streets; in Hamburg, radical left-wing autonomists are rioting. In societies around the world, the rifts are widening.

When I interviewed the former secretary of state Henry Kissinger in New York a few days after the 2016 presidential election, he talked of a possible civil war. I thought he was exaggerating. But with every passing month, the prospect seems more plausible. The people on both sides of the divide seem to have nothing left in common—except for maybe one thing: the wish for a solution. Yes, they have very different ideas about what the future of their country should look like, but most would agree that they don't want to see it broken. They want it to continue to exist, in stability and peace. But how?

The answer to that question must come from the politicians. But most of them, no matter which party they belong to, hide behind empty phrases. They talk of building bridges, of integrity, and of taking the fears and concerns of the people seriously. *Very well*, I always want to say, *but what does that mean? When you walk into the office at 9 AM and say, "Today I will really take the fears and concerns of the people seriously," what is the first thing you'll do? The second? The third?*

On the evening of September 3, 2017, I and sixteen million other viewers were watching the TV debate between the two main candidates in the upcoming elections for the German chancellorship. Just before 10 PM, Martin Schulz, at the time the leader of the Social Democrats and challenger to Angela Merkel, turned straight to the camera with a look heavy with meaning. The moderator, Maybrit Illner, had just asked him for his closing statement.

Schulz had known that this moment would come, that he, who sought to become chancellor during this major political crisis, would be able to give the people an uninterrupted address and present his solution. Presumably his speech writers and strategists had spent weeks fine-tuning every word that their candidate was about to utter and had practiced every artificial pause and every gesture underlining what was said. Then Schulz started to speak.

"We live in a time of turmoil," Schulz said in the tone of a lecture committed to memory but practiced inadequately. "And in times of turmoil, the best policy is to make a fresh start, and to have the courage to make a fresh start. The courage to make a fresh start means shaping the future, not managing the past."

I remember thinking, *He doesn't know what to do either.*

A few months later, Angela Merkel—reelected despite having offered nothing more substantial than her opponent—stood in front of the Bundestag, the German Federal Parliament, and explained how she was going to bring our divided society back together. She said she was going to adjust the exempt amount of income tax. She promised to introduce payments to help families buy their first home, twelve hundred euros for each child over ten. And she would lower the employment insurance tax. It reminded me of firefighters battling a forest fire with buckets, and I felt the same helplessness again, as if we were condemned to watch while the world around us was going up in flames.

Maybe it was by chance, or maybe it was my terrified subconscious, but I began to notice that in my work I was often meeting people who had overcome this sort of polarization. It may sound sappy, but the stories I encountered made me believe in the good in people. Sometimes I would write about it afterward, but it was only later that I realized that it was always the same mechanism that led to success, that sparked a certain magic.

Each time, enemies, opponents, and adversaries had met with each other. Each time, they had gotten to know each other well, not just superficially. And each time, they had come to think differently about each other, in a kinder, more nuanced, and intelligent way. In several cases, enemies had even become friends—sometimes best friends.

I began to ask myself: Might it be possible to develop what had occurred at the micro level into a strategy for the macro level, a political tool that could be used to rein in the centrifugal forces pulling on the liberal societies in the West?

It sounds like a megalomaniacal fantasy, I know. I spoke with political and social scientists—especially with social psychologists, including one who was clever enough to win a Nobel Prize in a field that wasn't even his own. I expected them to say, "Forget it, it'll never work," or to point out to me something that I had missed in my journalistic enthusiasm. But they didn't. Instead, I learned that this mighty mechanism I had discovered, the process that weakens hatred and brings animosities to an end, was first explained seventy years ago, that it had been scientifically researched. Yet as far as I could tell, this knowledge had never managed to make the jump from the academic to the real world, at least not on a significant scale. Wherever it had worked its magic, it had done so quietly, almost inadvertently. When I began searching for places where this mechanism may have been employed to intentionally overcome divisions, I realized that they exist too. But no one is looking.

This book *is* looking. It tells the stories of those places and their people. We will visit a village in Ireland, a police station in Denmark, and a school in Botswana. We will drink coffee in a row house in Hamburg, meet with neo-Nazis and Islamists, and with those who fight them. We will travel to the battlefields of World War II, and the Namibian desert. And we will dive into social-psychological experiments, the outcomes of which have made me see the world in a different light.

Before we set off, I want to promise two things. To all who— like me—tend to feel overwhelmed by the hatred spilling from their TV, newspapers, and Twitter feed: I promise that these pages will bring you hope, at least a little. And to all who—like me—are exasperated by their political representatives' hollow phrases that lack any real solutions: I promise that you will find the opposite here. You will find concrete first, second, and third steps that others have taken and that worked—and inspiration for what you can do to counteract hate.

1

The Others

How meeting with strangers can save society

Michael Kent would attack his victims with a baseball bat or with his fists. Wearing heavy boots, he would stomp on their heads and their motionless bodies. He would stab them with knives, and on at least one occasion, he had shot at people from a moving car. His friends called him Smiley because he smiled even as he dealt the blows. Almost all of Michael's victims were Black.

It was the 1990s, and Michael, although still a teenager, was a leader in the neo-Nazi scene in Phoenix, Arizona. He had a reputation for being fearless, for being ready to act when things needed to be done. And in his view, there was a lot to be done.

If it came to his attention that a Black man had approached a White woman, Michael would pick up a few friends, and together they would look for the man and beat him up. Sometimes they would follow him home and shoot at his house with assault rifles. If he learned that a White woman had responded to a Black man's advances, or, even worse, had initiated them herself, he would gather a few "skinbirds," as they called the women in their group, to beat up the "race traitor."

One night, when Michael was hanging out with a friend at a middle school in north Phoenix, he grabbed a gas can from his car and poured its contents onto the school sports field. Moments later, a huge swastika was burning in the darkness. Another time, one of his old friends told me, he drove his car into a young Black man walking on the sidewalk. From behind, without warning.

Today, Michael is in his early forties and lives in rural Arizona. He's asked me not to specify where exactly. A gravel path leads up to his house; his backyard borders the desert.

I meet him one evening in July 2021. As I pull up in his driveway in my rental car, the sun is setting, but it is still 120 degrees. Inside the house, the AC is keeping it nice and cool. Michael, in a white vest and shorts, is sitting on the sofa drinking beer. On his smartphone, he scrolls through photos from that time. Him doing the Hitler salute. Him posing in front of a swastika flag. Him with an AR-15-style rifle. Him in jail with fellow inmates, again doing the Hitler salute.

"Have you seen *American History X*?" Michael asks. "That was my life before the movie was even made."

The first time Michael was put behind bars was when, at the age of twelve, he was caught stealing condoms. He spent the following fifteen years in and out of jail, a few weeks' juvenile detention here, a few months' county jail there, and finally five years in prison. In order to survive inside, he says, you have to fall in with a crowd—in Arizona, *which* crowd is almost always determined by the color of your skin, he adds. From his first day in juvenile detention, he hung out with other White kids; it never occurred to him to do otherwise, he says today. Some of the guys were two or three years older and came from White supremacist families. Repeating the arguments made by their fathers and grandfathers, they explained to him that America was engaged in a "race war." White people were being attacked and had to fight back, they said. He, Michael, had to fight back.

He remembered that his mother had once narrowly escaped being raped by a Black intruder in her bedroom. She used to sleep with a 9mm handgun under the pillow and was able to scare him off. He remembered how, back in Pennsylvania where he lived at the time, the Black kids from next door used to beat him with sticks when he was playing in the woods behind the house. What the boys in prison were telling him now made sense. He had to fight back.

Michael doesn't remember the first Black person he beat up, but it must have been around the time he was in juvenile detention, he says—it was a common occurrence there. When he was a child, his mother had propped up a mattress in the basement and painted the silhouette of a person on it in black paint. That's how he learned to hit a target. Now he practiced on real people. What he was lacking in body mass he made up for in determination.

With every punch he delivered, with every kick he absorbed, Michael gained more respect from the other kids. Soon he had earned, letter by letter, his first tattoo. Using a guitar string, a fellow inmate tattooed the words WHITE PRIDE in red ink on his back, in a semicircle just below the neck. It was followed by a large black swastika on his chest. Then another on the back of his neck. Through the prison library he ordered books by David Duke, Joseph Goebbels, and Adolf Hitler. "I wanted to be like Hitler. He was one of the greatest leaders of all time."

On the rare occasions that Michael was not incarcerated during those years of his radicalization, he put what he had learned in prison into practice on the streets of Phoenix. He earned his living selling drugs. But mostly he spent his time hounding, beating, and knifing Black people, and attending neo-Nazi rallies. Today he says that he was lucky he never got busted doing the serious stuff, just for trivial things like being behind the wheel of a stolen Jeep Cherokee with a few grams of meth in each sock.

In the summer of 2006, Michael was released once more. He was twenty-seven years old and had no intention of changing his life. He moved into a trailer and hung confederate flags on his walls. A German war flag too. He had a portrait of Adolf Hitler engraved in the glass top of his kitchen table; he stuck a picture of the Führer in the rear window of his truck.

Then one day in the summer of 2007, he looked out his trailer window and saw a patrol car pull up outside his property. A woman got out, quite short, in her mid-thirties, wearing a uniform. On her belt Michael saw handcuffs and a gun. The woman was Black.

She walked up to the gate, rattling the fence with her baton, and his pit bull ran toward her. The woman pressed the back of her hand against the fence, and the dog started licking it. Then she opened the gate and walked toward the trailer. Michael stepped outside. The woman was only a couple of yards away, and he could read the white letters on her black body armor: PROBATION.

Tiffany Whittier was new in her job as a probation officer; Michael Kent was one of her first cases. Maybe that explains what today appears bold, perhaps even reckless: why she, a Black woman, went to see a neo-Nazi at his home, on her own. All she knew about him was what was in his file: that he had done time for theft, drug offenses, and contraband trade. She had seen a photo of the swastika tattoo on his chest but knew nothing about his history of violence.

Probation officers can drop in on their clients and enter their homes without notice. Tiffany says she used to do that a lot, especially for a first meeting. *Who else is there when you arrive? Do they stay when they see the patrol car pull up, or do they make a swift exit? Are they hurriedly stashing things away, like drug paraphernalia? What does the house smell like?* If the client doesn't know you're coming, you learn a lot more about them than by announcing yourself beforehand.

Michael's dog was friendly, even if it looked mean, Tiffany remembers. Then Michael stepped out of the trailer; he also looked mean. He was wearing a white tank top, a "wifebeater," she says. Underneath it she could glimpse the arms of the swastika on his chest.

As she remembers it, Michael asked, "Who are you?"

"I'm Tiffany, your probation officer," she replied.

Michael looked around. "Are you by yourself?"

Tiffany took a step back and placed her right hand on her gun.

"Yes," she said. "Is there a problem?"

"No," Michael said and walked up to her. "I have respect for you."

Previously, his probation officers had mostly been men and had always come in teams of at least two. He could tell that they were afraid of him. And now this Black woman had the guts to show up on her own. He reached out his hand, and Tiffany shook it.

Tiffany followed Michael inside. At the door she noticed his black combat boots, placed neatly side by side. The laces were red, indicating in neo-Nazi circles that the owner of the boots had spilled the blood of a perceived enemy of the White race. On his walls were Confederate flags, and a black, white, and red flag, which she later learned was the German war flag from the Nazi era. A swastika and the image of Adolf Hitler were engraved in his kitchen table. She ignored all of it.

Today Tiffany says that she concentrated on what she had been taught. *Is there any drug paraphernalia lying around? Are there any weapons on display? Any knives, blades?* She saw none of that. Michael's home was astonishingly clean.

They made some small talk, neither of them can remember what about. She set up an appointment for her next visit and gave him a piece of paper that said what fees he would have to pay, and when. Her visit lasted only a few minutes.

"Driving away, I remember thinking it went better than expected," Tiffany tells me.

Every day on her way to work, Tiffany drove past Michael's place of work, a chicken farm. Most days, she would see his truck parked there, with the Hitler sticker on the back. One time she stopped and went inside, and Michael introduced her to his boss. Michael appeared to be a hard worker.

"I knew I was supposed to hate Tiffany, but for some reason I didn't," Michael recalls.

He paid his monthly probation fees, and he was on time for his appointments. He treated her with respect. Once, during an unannounced visit at his home, she found a knife with a swastika engraved in the handle. She confiscated it but let it go at that. Another time he opened the door drunk. If she caught him drinking again, she told him, she'd have to report it. When she did catch him again, she sent him to see a therapist.

They never discussed politics, never mentioned the color of her skin or the clashing contrast between them. They talked about trivial things, and as the months went by, Michael talked more, while Tiffany listened. Michael talked about the problems with his new girlfriend, who was taking drugs. About the fact that when he couldn't put up with it any longer, he'd throw a mattress onto the flatbed of his truck and drive to a nearby mountain to spend the night up there. When one of his best friends died, he called Tiffany. At times her work cell phone would ring so often that she stopped answering it.

Before he met Tiffany, Michael had never actually had a proper conversation with a Black person. Now it was a Black woman who gave him what he never even knew he needed. He opened up; he cried in front of her. It had been drilled into him his whole life that he mustn't show any kind of weakness. Now he did just that, and it felt good.

With tears in his eyes, Michael tells me, "She was Black, but I didn't look at her as being Black. I saw her for who she was. That woke something up inside of me."

During one of her visits to Michael's trailer, Tiffany pointed to one of the flags on the walls and asked, "Why don't you take this negative stuff down and put up some smiley faces instead?" She says she meant it as a joke, but by her next visit Michael had actually put up a poster with smileys. He had packed the flags away, and in the yard behind the house he had smashed the glass top of his kitchen table with a baseball bat.

Tiffany encouraged Michael to buy a house, which he did—in her neighborhood. When he said to his girlfriend, "You're fat, stop eating so much," it was Tiffany who told him that it was inappropriate. When he got married, she attended as a guest, the only Black person in a sea of White people, some of whom were active neo-Nazis. Michael told the other guests, "She is a friend."

In 2010, Tiffany recommended that Michael's probation period be reduced because he had turned his life around. The court agreed, and Tiffany gave Michael her private cell phone number. A few months later, Michael's wife gave birth to his son, Michael Jr. Michael and his son would often drop by to see Tiffany; the boy called her "girlfriend."

For a long time, Michael Kent's life had been governed by ideology. Apart from the routine violence and the constant fear of being arrested, his racist beliefs had controlled every minute detail of his existence. For example, he would only eat out at a restaurant once he had established that all the waiters and kitchen staff were White. For a time, he grew his own vegetables because he didn't want to eat anything from a store that might have been touched by Black or Mexican field workers. And he found a new auto repair shop after he realized that the mechanic who had fixed his truck was Black.

After meeting Tiffany, he says, all this effort, this stress, this hatred felt increasingly absurd to him, sometimes downright ridiculous. At some point, Michael says, he just let go. He walked away. And it was surprisingly easy.

He distanced himself from most of his friends. After separating from his wife, he started dating again. "Since then, I've been dating almost exclusively outside my race," he says, scrolling through pictures of Black and Brown women. He also got in touch with an old crush from his high school days, a Mexican woman named Melissa. Eventually Michael moved houses, fearing that his old friends might come after him, a traitor in their eyes.

In September 2017, Michael walked into a tattoo studio and got a huge bear tattoo over his entire chest, to cover up the swastika. Since then, he and Tiffany have been traveling all over America, giving interviews and speeches.

On Martin Luther King Jr. Day in 2019, they went to Atlanta. King's daughter Bernice had invited them to get up onstage with her and speak. Tiffany says that her grandmother had often talked about attending King's famous speech in Washington, DC, in 1963. So this day, she says, felt incredibly special to her.

"What Martin Luther King Jr. wanted was for people to all accept each other, you know, not based off the color of your skin. And so here I was with Michael. It was just, I don't know how to put it in words, it was so heartwarming. It was amazing. But I was more excited for Michael, I really was. For him it's like 180 degrees from hate to love."

• • •

Michael's story reminds me of someone else, a man named Harald, who lives thousands of miles away in Hamburg, Germany's second-largest city, just a few minutes from my own home, in fact. When I first met Harald a few years ago, he was in his seventies, and he had been living in fear for some time. At the height of the so-called "refugee crisis," he saw on TV how hundreds of thousands of migrants were pouring into the country, from Iraq, Syria, and Afghanistan, but also Roma people from the Balkans.

As a young boy, in the 1940s, his parents had warned him: "Harald, beware of the gypsies, they steal blond children." As a teenager, in the 1950s, he says he witnessed Roma people, which he offensively refers to as gypsies, in Hamburg going from door to door, trying to sell their junk to the Germans. As an adult, in the 1960s, he says he noticed that it was often gypsies who were getting into fights at the bar on the corner. That's why all these refugees coming into Germany now only meant one thing to him: trouble.

Harald Hermes and his wife, Christa, live on the ground floor of a row house on the outskirts of Hamburg. The two-bedroom apartment has been their home for almost fifty years. Outside, the brick façade has faded; inside, the apartment has taken on that grandparent-y feel that comes with flowery curtains, ornaments on the windowsills, and crocheted doilies protecting the precious coffee table. The photos on the walls show two smiling daughters, both mothers themselves now. After Harald Hermes gave up his job as a car mechanic in 2001, he worked a few more years as a janitor. After he retired, he says all his days were kind of the same: Get up, eat breakfast, eat lunch, sometimes go to a doctor's appointment in the morning, or receive a visit from the grandchildren in the afternoon.

But over the years, many of their neighbors, retirees like them, had died. The apartments stood empty, and in the spring of 2014, the first refugees arrived. A German neighbor called the local council to complain. Another turned to the local newspaper. Harald Hermes wrote letters to the local government and to the political parties. To no effect. Afghani families moved into the area, followed by Macedonians and Roma. After years of silence on the lawns between the apartment blocks, the sound of children playing was a nuisance. The stairwells echoed with incomprehensible languages. The balconies were draped in rugs and foreign garments, even though the regulations explicitly forbade the drying of laundry on the balconies. Harald Hermes recorded these transgressions with his digital camera and emailed the photos to the property manager. Again, to no effect.

That summer, during Ramadan, many of their new Muslim neighbors lit barbecues on their balconies after the sun had set. Christa and Harald Hermes remember lying in bed, unable to sleep, as throaty sounds of foreign languages and the smell of barbecued meat drifted through their open window. In the winter, with temperatures below freezing, the new neighbors' windows were wide open, with the heat on full blast. Harald Hermes wrote to Olaf Scholz, then the mayor of Hamburg, and to Wolfgang Schäuble, the finance minister. Harald Hermes had seen him on TV saying something like, "No one would have to pay one bit extra because of the refugees." But here he was, with an extra five hundred euros on the gas meter.

Harald Hermes didn't want any foreigners in Germany, and now that some had moved in, he felt his views had been validated. The Hermeses considered themselves lucky at first: The early refugees had moved into the other apartment blocks, and they had always had at least one area of grass between them and the large, noisy families. In the beginning, the only ones living in their block were an elderly Afghani couple, who were quiet and always said a friendly "Hello." The apartment immediately above the Hermeses', where the Albrechts had lived for over forty years, stood empty.

That is, until one day in April, when Christa Hermes was on her balcony and noticed a few people lurking around the apartment block next door. A brawny young man. A pretty woman with long black hair, a baby in her arms. Between them, three more children, none taller than an adult's waist. Christa Hermes saw the strangers' searching gaze come to a halt on the balcony above her head and watched them make their way slowly across the grass. She turned and called through the open balcony door to her husband inside: "Harald, I think we're getting gypsies!"

The family stopped underneath Christa Hermes's balcony and looked up. Harald had come out too. The young woman introduced all six of them, names that Christa Hermes immediately forgot. Then the couple watched the family step through the front door. Through the thin walls, they could hear them climb the stairs. Once inside their new apartment, the children were running around from one room to the next, tap, tap, tap, and back again, tap, tap, tap. That evening, the Hermeses had to turn up the volume on the TV.

The next day, water was dripping onto the Hermes' balcony. Christa went upstairs and rang the bell. A child opened the door, followed shortly by the woman. "There's water coming from your balcony," Christa Hermes said, but the woman didn't understand.

"Can you speak English?" the woman asked, but Christa Hermes didn't understand. So she pushed past the woman and the child and marched through the apartment to the balcony door. Outside, she found onesies, pants, and towels hanging on a line, sopping wet.

"You can't do that," Christa Hermes said.

The woman led Christa Hermes to the bathroom and pointed to the tub. Now Christa Hermes understood. The woman had no washing machine, no dryer, and no drying rack. As a child, Christa Hermes had to wash the laundry by hand too, and now she remembered the calluses on her hands. Christa was able to explain that she had a spare drying rack in the basement, and asked if the woman would like to have it. The woman said she would.

On the way back to the door, Christa Hermes glanced around the apartment. Two cups sat on the table, and on the stovetop an empty can of beans, which looked like it had been used to heat up baby food. There didn't appear to be any dishes. Also, it was far too warm even for a sunny April day like this one. Christa Hermes pointed questioningly to a radiator, and the woman explained in broken German that the children were cold at night in their beds. She said they didn't have blankets or pillows, only their pajamas.

"That's when a lightbulb went on in my head," Christa Hermes remembers.

Later that day, she shuttled up and down the stairs, back and forth between the apartment and the basement. She brought woolen blankets and pillows and bed linen, she hauled dishes, pots and pans, a kettle, and an old coffee machine that still worked. Soon she was drinking coffee with the woman, whose name was Rosi,[1] she had learned, and little Milan was climbing onto her lap. Then Harald joined them, and he was told that in Serbia, Robert, Rosi's husband, had trained as a car mechanic: They had the same trade.

From then on, Rosi used the Hermeses' clothesline on the lawn. When Christa had the time—and she often did—she helped Rosi hang up the laundry. Sometimes she went upstairs for a cuddle with the children, who had started calling her Grandma. When Milan, who had so much energy, was too wild, Rosi admonished him: "Shh! Grandpa sleeping downstairs."

Rosi and Robert were soon calling Christa "Mommy." It irritated her at first, but then she learned that both had grown up in broken homes where they had experienced little kindness but plenty of violence. Apart from themselves, Rosi and Robert say, Christa Hermes was the only person who had ever shown love to the children.

In the summer, they went on a trip to the river Elbe together. It was warm, and Rosi, up to her knees in the water, was knocked over by a wave. They laughed about it. Rosi cooked a spicy meal, which even Harald ate, even though he doesn't really like spicy food. For Anastasia's first day at school, Christa Hermes baked a strawberry cake with lots of fresh strawberries. Within a few weeks, the "gypsies" had become people: Robert, Rosi, Milan, Anastasia, Christina, and Monika. They were soon the Hermeses' closest friends.

Three years later, I am sitting in the Hermeses' living room. Harald Hermes shakes his head, still incredulous: "We can't really explain it ourselves." Christa adds: "That the heart can be so full of love for strangers. We couldn't imagine it. It's not like it was prescribed or something, it just happened."

The Hermeses filled a hole in the lives of "their Serbs," as they soon called their neighbors. They showed them around Hamburg, explained Germany to them. And "their Serbs" filled a hole in the Hermeses' lives, who hadn't realized how much they were longing to be needed. Sometimes Harald Hermes wonders what their lives would have looked like if Christa hadn't gone upstairs to complain that day. If Christa hadn't seen that these people had been put into that apartment by the council with little more than the clothes on their backs. If she hadn't understood that her neighbors had not hung their laundry on the balcony out of laziness, ignorance, or spite, but because they had no other choice.

At the end of August, Harald went with Robert to see a lawyer in the city center. "Asylum won't be granted," said the lawyer. So Harald wrote another letter to the government, this time to the immigration authority. *Germany could use a tradesman like Robert*, he wrote. The family was willing to integrate, adopt German values, and he, Harald Hermes, could vouch for that. They had even raised a German flag, and were fans of the HSV, Hamburg's soccer team.

Just as Michael Kent had spoken out in favor of equality, eager to help the people he once used to hate, Harald Hermes was trying to prevent a deportation that six months earlier he would have heartily supported, back when the new neighbor was a problem, a potential crook or a thug, a gypsy. But then he turned out to be a diligent worker, a caring father—yes, still a Roma, as Harald Hermes calls them now, but a very likeable one.

In early September, the Hermeses traveled to Austria to celebrate their golden wedding anniversary. On their way home, they stopped over with Harald's sister in the Westerwald region of Germany. They were enjoying afternoon coffee on the patio when Harald's cell phone rang. Christa could make out Rosi's voice. Then she saw tears rolling down her husband's cheeks—Harald, who never cried. She knew right away.

Rosi was calling from a park bench in Belgrade, Serbia. The police had come for them in the night.

Back in Hamburg, the Hermeses used their spare key and packed their neighbors' belongings, many of which had previously been their own, into suitcases and boxes, and shipped them to Serbia. The Hermeses raised money from others and donated some of their own money to the Serbian family. They installed Skype and Telegram on their tablet and spoke every day with the family, who had moved into a small house with a leaking roof and an adjoining pigpen two hours north of Belgrade. A few months later, the Hermeses boarded a plane—a first for Christa, who has a paralyzing fear of flying. They stayed a week. In the following three years, they would return six more times, once with a car they purchased for their Serbs in Hamburg, driving over a thousand miles in two days. When I first met them, four years after the family was deported, the Hermeses were still sending them food and toys, and money for furniture, tools, and firewood. Despite the long distance, the Hermeses kept in touch with them more than they did with their own children. And lately, Christa Hermes had been haunted by a recurring thought that, she says, sometimes kept her awake at night: *What if I never see them again?*

• • •

A few months earlier, at the height of the German refugee crisis, my editor had sent me to a village in the mountainous south of Germany, where the state government of Baden-Württemberg had converted an empty army barracks into a reception center for asylum seekers. The barracks was located on the edge of a village called Messstetten, a picture-postcard paradise of single-family homes, with meticulously kept front yards and expensive cars parked in the driveways. Thousands of refugees had recently moved in, and the internet was running wild with outrageous stories. Asylum seekers were reported to have stolen goats and molested women. The latest rumor claimed that the farmer whose land was adjacent to the barracks had found a severed head in his trash can.

Gerold Huber greeted me in a broad Swabian dialect and with a firm handshake. As he showed me around the farm, walking past the stables and an idling tractor, I saw refugees strolling around the barracks behind the fence. I asked him about the severed head, and he replied that it had never happened. Like most news spread on Facebook, he added, it was fake. And then he told me a story.

Gerold Huber had been against housing refugees in the barracks. He had voiced his concerns to the regional government: With thousands of Muslims, many of them traumatized by war, he was worried for his children, who were six, nine, and twelve years old at the time. The refugees came anyway, most of them from Syria and Iraq—indeed, from societies torn apart by violence. Sometimes a few of them would come and ask for milk. He let them have some. Once, he gave a lift in his car to a pregnant woman who had been left on the curb by her traffickers.

The more Huber talked with refugees, he now admits, the more he came to realize: Most of them were nice people. The two or three police incidents at the barracks were no longer of any concern to him. Soon he didn't object to his daughter going over there with her friends to help the refugee children with their German homework. His wife also volunteered her time. He wrote to the district office again, this time suggesting that they organize shuttle buses. The refugees had to walk over a mile to the village for their groceries. He was proud when the buses arrived.

Like Michael Kent and Harald Hermes, Gerold Huber took a stand for those whom he had rejected at first. He too transformed his perspective of those people. Potential criminals posing a threat to his children became pleasant neighbors who had to lug their heavy grocery bags along a busy road. He had cultivated his fears from a distance, had formed prejudices and, like the neo-Nazi from Phoenix, and the couple from Hamburg, changed his views when he saw that they were wrong.

This fascinated me, because it seemed to go against the zeitgeist. In America, you were either conservative or liberal, for Trump or against; either you supported equality for people of all colors or you feared it as a threat to your own group. In Germany, at the height of the refugee crisis, it was a similar story. The public debate seemed to demand a decision by each individual: Either you are for the refugees or you are against them. Either you label them as "desperate" or as "dangerous." Once they had made up their mind, most people seemed to stick by their decision. Not Michael Kent, not Harald and Christa Hermes. Not Gerold Huber.

When I started telling my friends about these people, they often said something along the lines of: *How wonderful that people who are open enough to overcome their prejudices exist! And what a lovely coincidence that these people met.* Their tone suggested that these people must be special, more open and caring than others, possessing a rare amount of empathy, living undetected in our midst until they are exposed by some chance event.

Then I kept coming across such caring people. I read about an anti-abortionist from California who changed his views after talking to a woman who explained why she'd gotten an abortion. I read about Israeli and Palestinian youths who had become friends during a three-week camping trip. I read a book by the Black musician Daryl Davis, who used to play piano in a bar. One night, one of the customers, a member of the Ku Klux Klan, was so moved by his music that he approached Davis that very evening. Over the weeks that followed they became friends, and the man soon left the Klan. The people in these stories could be seen as "natural" enemies. But when they met, it didn't end badly, as one would expect. The opposite occurred.

One hot summer day in 2018, I stepped onto a restaurant patio in the northeastern German town of Wismar and found waiting for me a beefy man with tattooed arms, a big beard, and a shaved head: Sven Krüger, a neo-Nazi.

• • •

In my job as a reporter, I sometimes meet extreme people. That day, I interviewed Sven Krüger for a feature that would later appear in the weekly German newspaper *Die Zeit* where I work. Krüger has spent ten years in jail and was once a member of the regional parliament for the extreme right-wing National Democratic Party of Germany, the NPD. He participated in the 1992 anti-migrant riots in Rostock-Lichtenhagen, something he is still proud of, he tells me. During the interview, he talks about his nationalist, *völkisch*, views, about blood and ancestral lines, and about his vision for a national-socialist Germany. It is disturbing to listen to him. Krüger expresses the most racist views, not in a self-conscious whisper, but proudly, and in such a loud voice that I look around, embarrassed, to see if anyone's listening. An hour in, the conversation gets interesting as Krüger talks about an experience he had in jail.

A few cells down from his there was a Palestinian, he tells me, using the derogatory term *Kanake*. During yard exercise, they eyed each other like enemies. At the time, Krüger was in his mid-thirties and used to work out a lot, especially bench presses. The prison gym had a bench press. It was perfect, really, except that you need a partner to use it, in case the bar slips. Unfortunately, there was only one other regular visitor to the gym: the Palestinian.

So Krüger did pull-ups and push-ups instead—until one day, when he saw the Palestinian struggling under a large weight on the bench, by himself. Krüger went over to him and held his fingers under the bar, signaling, "I am here if anything goes wrong." Afterward, Krüger lay down on the bench, and the Palestinian returned the favor. Not a word passed between them, Krüger says. Not long after, they were both assigned to the same work gang. Side by side, they swept their sector and scrubbed the kitchen in silence.

On the patio, Krüger can't remember who spoke first, only that it was in the break room and that the Palestinian was ranting about Israel, about how his family had been living in a refugee camp for two generations. Krüger says he replied, "I don't like the Jews either." Suddenly, his enemy's enemy had become his friend—and remained so for the rest of their jail term. "It was a significant moment because he was the first Palestinian I'd really gotten to know," Krüger says. "Like when you're lying in a trench in World War I, the Germans on one side, the French on the other, and at Christmas they put up a Christmas tree together. A little isolated peace, on the spur of the moment. That's what it felt like for me."

Later, I am unable to verify the story because I cannot track down the Palestinian inmate. But talking about him in Wismar and noticing my surprise, Krüger tells me another story, one from 2001.

Peter Cipra, a restaurant owner from Wismar, had a crazy idea. He was fed up with the regular street fights between clashing left- and right-wing extremists in his city. Unhappy with the fact that Wismar only ever made the news in connection with violence and neo-Nazis, Peter wanted to do something. He was a fan of extreme travel, so he decided to take two left-wing punks and two neo-Nazis on a trip to Namibia to spend six weeks hiking through the desert together.

One of the neo-Nazis was Sven Krüger, the other a buddy of Sven's whom he had introduced to Peter. They would not know who the other two were until they met them at the train station on their way to the airport: two punks, with matted hair and torn clothes. It turned out that Krüger had once smashed a bottle of sparkling wine over one of their heads. The other had hit him in the face with a motorbike helmet. One of them was twenty-three-year-old Thomas Wahnig. On the train, Krüger passed around beer and cigarettes.

In Namibia they walked through the desert, up to twenty miles a day, with temperatures often in the hundreds. In the evenings, sitting around the fire and tired from the efforts of the day, the two punks turned out to be quite nice. The small group was led by Haruendo, the son of a chieftain of the Himba people, who wore nothing but a loincloth and a dagger in a belt. To protect against malaria, he would rub his skin and hair with a mixture of red clay and cow dung as a mosquito repellent. Haruendo was the only one who knew where the waterholes were. They would often drink brown sludge, which Haruendo would dig up from the ground. After a week, Thomas started vomiting blood. He was barely able to stand, but it wasn't his punk buddy who took care of him. It was Sven Krüger, the most infamous neo-Nazi of northern Germany, Wahnig's enemy, who was toting Thomas's backpack through the desert.

Today, Thomas Wahnig is in his mid-forties and lives in a village in the Mecklenburg region of northern Germany. He tells me that before the Namibia trip his life had been defined by two aims: to get hold of beer every day, by breaking into supermarkets with his friends, if necessary, and to beat up neo-Nazis. The encounter with Krüger transformed his life, he says. On his return home, Wahnig broke with his punk friends, cut his hair, and swapped his boots for sneakers. Today he is married, with six children. His views are still very much on the left, but in his house he has a wall with pictures of the Namibia trip. When the children ask about the tattooed skinhead in the photos, he tells them about Sven, the neo-Nazi who helped him. And about how someone's political outlook does not necessarily tell you what kind of person they are. That neo-Nazis can be nice people.

That realization, which, he says, for him as a radical leftist was extremely uncomfortable at first, has shaped and liberated his thinking: that someone's personality is never one-dimensional. But do a person's distasteful characteristics outweigh the pleasant ones? What is more important, Sven Krüger's racism or his helpfulness? His political views or his private nature? Wahnig says, "Politically, I still think that Sven is completely wrong. But, as a person, I like him."

Back in Germany, telling his buddies about his Africa trip, Sven Krüger would sometimes mention the nights spent around the fire with the two punks. More often than not, however, he would talk about the Africans he had observed sitting idly by the roadside or leaning against their mopeds instead of working. Now that Krüger had seen them with his own eyes, he could, with some authority, call them lazy. But for him there was one exception: Haruendo.

After the group had been traveling for just over a week, and Thomas Wahnig had already been forced to quit, exhausted by heat, exertion, and dirty water, Peter Cipra, the initiator of the trip, passed out. Krüger and Haruendo strapped him to the back of a donkey and they made their way to the nearest hospital. Suspected diagnosis: malaria. While Cipra was recovering, Krüger and Haruendo spent the days together. Shading from the sun under a tree, they "philosophized about living and letting live," Krüger remembers. Haruendo took him hunting for antelope and fishing for catfish. Seventeen years later, on the restaurant patio in Wismar, Krüger tells me about Haruendo, and it sounds as if he's talking about a long-lost friend from his childhood.

A punk in the habit of beating up neo-Nazis meets one and likes him. A Muslim-hating neo-Nazi who despises lefties and considers people of color inferior becomes friends with a Palestinian, carries a punk's backpack through the desert, and goes fishing with a Himba. How is that possible? When I put the question to Sven Krüger, he replies, "The problem is, once you actually get to know them, you can no longer hate them."

Apparently, this rare group of kind and caring people not only includes Michael Kent, Christa and Harald Hermes, Gerold Huber, the California anti-abortionist, the Israeli and Palestinian youths, the musician Daryl Davis and his Ku Klux Klan friend, but also the ex-punk Thomas Wahnig and the neo-Nazi Sven Krüger. Either this group is bigger than I thought, or the truth is much more mundane: There is no such group.

Maybe my friends were wrong. Maybe the coincidence wasn't that the *right* kind of people met each other, but that the right kind of people *met*. Maybe it's not the people who make these stories stand out; maybe it's the circumstances.

• • •

When was the last time you spoke to somebody completely different from you, or to somebody who holds completely different opinions? I don't mean small talk with your right-leaning uncle last Thanksgiving, or a few polite exchanges with the cashier at the supermarket. I'm talking about a deep, meaningful conversation. It doesn't happen very often; our daily lives don't usually allow for it.

On my way to the office, I always bike along the same route through the streets of Hamburg. Sometimes it feels as if the traffic lights are in sync with my movements. Without thinking about it, my speed is such that I arrive at the junction just as the lights turn green. It makes me happy every time. The beauty of routine lies in its reliability, and I am not alone in this. We congratulate ourselves on how free we are in our modern industrial societies, but our existence is based on constant repetition.

The alarm goes off at the same time every morning. In the car, we hope the traffic won't make us late for work. Later, we rush home to be back in time for kickoff, a dinner date, a bedtime story with the kids, in houses, streets, and neighborhoods where everyone is in the same boat. Our daily routine leaves time for only a few people: family at the breakfast table, fellow commuters on the train, colleagues in the lunchroom, friends we might go see a movie with.

These few people tend to have similar jobs, a similar income, the same hobbies, and they are likely to vote for the same party. It is easy to understand why we surround ourselves with people who are like us; anything else would be hard work. The music on our car radio is tailored by an algorithm to a target group that we are part of. Facebook feeds us personalized ads. Amazon knows which books we might like. All of that is very comfortable and consistent.

Our individualized modern lives are such that we spend every day, every week, every year with the same people holding the same views repeating the same sequence of steps, as sure-footed as a professional dancer in a well-rehearsed choreography. We consign the unknown, the strange, the adventure to a two-week window in our schedule and call it "vacation." That is fair enough, and it wouldn't be a problem if this familiar merry-go-round didn't lead us to confuse our own limited horizons with reality. Reality includes the people not traveling on our commuter train and not having lunch in our cafeteria; it includes those who earn much more than we do and those who earn much less; those who listen to different radio stations, who see different ads on Facebook and different book suggestions on Amazon; those who vote for other parties but who all live in the same city, the same country. They are our fellow citizens, and yet they remain strangers. Ignoring them comes so naturally to us that we look at the red-and-blue maps on election night and ask ourselves: *Who are these people?*

This segregation of the social spheres is brought about not just by political decision-making and technological innovation; social progress shares the blame. With women represented at (nearly) all professional levels, a male senior physician is now less likely to marry a nurse and more likely to marry another senior physician; likewise, a male attorney is now more likely to marry another attorney than a secretary.

In this bubble-based society, there is a lot of distance and very little communication between the many groups, between rich and poor, young and old, immigrants and natives. It's the perfect breeding ground for prejudice. Michael Kent belonged to such a bubble. He had never had a proper conversation with a Black person and wanted to keep it that way—until Tiffany Whittier showed up at his door, and he had to engage with her. Christa and Harald Hermes belonged to a bubble too—until those they resented moved in upstairs. So did Gerold Huber—until suddenly a thousand refugees became his neighbors. And Sven Krüger—until he found himself literally confined with his enemies, in a prison, in the desert.

They had no choice. These strange and foreign "others" plunged into their lives, and suddenly their fears and prejudices fell apart. They came face-to-face with reality. It was uncomfortable, but impossible to ignore. Could it be that we might all experience a similar "disillusionment" if we step out of our bubble? That the only reason we don't know is because it happens so rarely?

• • •

When a group of GIs stepped out of the woods in the early hours of March 7, 1945, and saw before them the German town of Remagen, they could scarcely believe their eyes. As the morning fog lifted over the river Rhine, the Ludendorff bridge was revealed—it was still standing. All the other bridges had been blown up by the retreating Nazis to prevent the advancing Americans from crossing their last great obstacle. But here the soldiers had a clear view of the thousand-foot-long steel construction that led straight across to the other side—a godsend and a death trap, for on the eastern bank they could make out Wehrmacht soldiers frantically running to and fro, apparently preparing the demolition.

The American commanders ordered their men onto the bridge. As the soldiers crouched forward, artillery shells exploded around them and volleys of gunfire erupted from the other side. Climbing over the bodies of their fallen comrades, a few men made it across. Others followed. They established the bridgehead and stormed surrounding hills. They dug themselves in and waited for backup.

Adolf Hitler issued orders to drive the Americans back, and one of the last major battles of World War II ensued. The Wehrmacht deployed unit after unit in the battle for the bridgehead, which was defended by K Company, among others. Many of K company's soldiers had already died, and many others were wounded. If backup didn't arrive soon, they would be overrun by the Germans. At last, on March 13, 1945, they heard gunfire coming from the woods below their position. The author David P. Colley, who later interviewed the veterans and reconstructed the events of that day, described the moment: "When the firing finally died down, the Americans feared the worst, and the sound of men approaching only increased their apprehension. As a ragged line of soldiers began emerging from the woods, ducking under the low branches of the firs and hardwoods, the men of K Company hunkered down in their foxholes, gripping their weapons and straining to get a good look. To their relief, they could soon see that the advancing men were clad in olive drab and wore American pot-like helmets. However, as the approaching troops came closer, the GIs in K Company saw that their faces were brown and seemed to merge with the mud color of their helmets. Their relief was quickly displaced by shock. . . . Coming to their aid were Black Americans, and—even more startling—these Black soldiers were there not simply to relieve them but to join them in battle."[2]

For the first time since the Revolutionary War, the US Army broke with its policy of segregation during the final phase of World War II. Many White Americans still considered Black

Americans to be less intelligent, more violent, more sexually uninhibited, and lazier and dirtier than themselves. In parts of the country, there were laws prohibiting Black people and White people from studying in the same schools, traveling on the same buses, dining in the same restaurants, or sleeping in the same hotels. Naturally, they were not allowed to fight side by side. In a letter to his wife, General George S. Patton wrote, "[A] colored soldier cannot think fast enough to fight in armor.[3]"

In the eyes of the US Army, allowing Black soldiers and White soldiers to fight alongside each other would have prevented the unit from bonding as a "band of brothers." Where mutual trust meant the difference between life and death, they feared there would be distrust. Therefore, the few Black soldiers who served in army units were organized in their own, separate Black platoons—until that day on the right bank of the Rhine, when the war left the army no alternative. The battles incurred heavy losses, and the only soldiers who were available to help were Black.

One of those Black soldiers, J. Cameron Wade, later commented: "We ate together, slept together, fought together. There were no incidents. The Army couldn't believe it."[4] They held the riverbank; then they marched toward the East, toward victory.

The war had created a social experiment. Out of sheer necessity, a tiny part of American society—a few thousand GIs in the muddy hills of the Rhineland—had given up racial segregation. To understand the effect this had on those involved, the US Army sent researchers to survey the soldiers. General Patton may have been surprised by the result: 77 percent of the White soldiers who had fought alongside their Black counterparts said that they now "felt more respect for them" and "liked them better." Before the battle, they had considered them cowards; the officers had assumed that Black soldiers under fire would run away. Asked afterward how well the Black soldiers had performed in combat, 84 percent of the respondents answered, "Very well," and the remaining 16 percent said, "Well."[5] A company commander from Nevada commented, "You might think that wouldn't work well, but it did." A platoon sergeant from South Carolina admitted, "When we saw how they fought, I changed my mind." And a platoon commander from Texas said, "We all expected trouble. Haven't had any."[6]

For the soldiers, the war had the same effect the probation obligations had on Michael Kent or the sudden arrival of new neighbors on the Hermeses and Gerold Huber: It forced them to come eye to eye with reality, with the humanity of the other. It smashed their prejudices. Thanks to the army survey, we know that it wasn't just a few individual GIs who changed their mind, not just some special, rare, empathic soldiers. In fact, it was the vast majority.

After the war, the results of the survey found their way onto Gordon W. Allport's desk at Harvard University. Allport, one of the most extraordinary social psychologists of the twentieth century, was working on a book about prejudice. Growing up in Ohio, he had been bullied by his classmates for being born with only eight toes. Allport was terrible at sports but a brilliant student. He achieved top grades, became editor of his high school newspaper, and delivered his class's graduation speech. He went to Harvard on a scholarship and eventually became professor of social psychology.

Now, Allport's head was bent over the army survey. In the last few months of the war, the people involved in the study had not only questioned the GIs who actually fought alongside their Black comrades but had in fact interviewed seventeen hundred US soldiers throughout various countries in Europe and some who had remained stateside.[7] They had always asked the same question: "Some Army divisions have companies which include Black and white platoons. How would you feel about it if your outfit was set up something like that?"

It may help to use a comparison to simplify things: Let's imagine there are four groups of White soldiers. The first group consists of the men who actually fought at the Ludendorff bridge alongside their Black counterparts. The second group are the men on the opposite side of the river who had nothing to do with the Black soldiers but who might have observed the battle through binoculars. The third consists of soldiers from fifty miles behind the frontline who had only heard about the battle on their radios. And the final group are the soldiers who never left the United States, maybe because they were still in training. Let's imagine that all four groups were asked the same question: "Would you mind very much serving in the same platoon as Black soldiers?"

Of the soldiers in the fourth group, those who hadn't shipped out, 62 percent said that they "would dislike it very much." These soldiers had never had anything to do with Black people. Of the soldiers fifty miles behind the frontline, who had heard of the deployment of the Black soldiers, only 24 percent gave that answer. A large majority did not dislike the idea. Of the soldiers on the other side of the Rhine, who had witnessed the battle, only 20 percent disliked it. And among those who had experienced it firsthand, it was only 7 percent. Seven percent! Their prejudices had been blown to smithereens on the battlefield.

The closer the contact, the less prejudice there was as a result. Does that apply generally? Or does the context only apply to ethnic prejudice? Maybe it was the exceptional circumstances; after all, these soldiers were involved in the bloodiest war in history. Isn't it normal that people ignore each other's skin color when they're fighting a common enemy, when their own lives are at stake? Gordon Allport probably pondered the same question when studying the results—but then he found a second set of data in the army survey.

Given that they were already in the field, the army researchers didn't stop at asking the soldiers about their Black comrades. They also questioned them about another group of people: the enemy, the Germans. Among men who had never set foot in Germany, 36 percent reported that they had a favorable opinion of German people. Of the soldiers who had been in Germany within the last three days but had had no contact with the civilian population, it was already 49 percent. Of those who had had a couple of hours' contact with German civilians, it rose to 57 percent, and among those with more than five hours' contact, it was 76 percent.[8]

Let's let that sink in. The frontline soldiers predominantly had a favorable opinion of the population of the country against which they were fighting the biggest war in history. It was the same story: The closer the contact, the less prejudice and the more sympathy prevailed.

There was no need for a common enemy, no life-or-death situation. Contact alone did the trick. Now, you might argue that in both cases it was soldiers who overcame their bias; who knows if the same mechanism works in civilian life?

Allport discovered a study involving a high school class from Ohio.[9] Before they set off on a school trip in 1941, twenty-seven students were asked to rate their classmates from 1 ("Would have as my best friend") to 7 ("Would rather have them miles away"). They spent a week in Chicago visiting the Federal Reserve Bank, the stockyards and slaughterhouses, and the Ford assembly plant. They shared hotel rooms and sat down together for three meals each day. Upon their return, they were asked to fill out the same questionnaire again. Twenty of the twenty-seven students were now more popular than before. Here again, close contact had led to prejudices being abandoned, and the class had become closer as a result.

Allport published his findings under the title *The Nature of Prejudice* in 1954, at a time of great political upheaval, which he describes in his preface: "Muslims distrust non-Muslims. Jews who escaped extermination in Central Europe find themselves in the new State of Israel surrounded by anti-Semitism. Refugees roam in inhospitable lands. . . . While some of this endless antagonism seems based upon a realistic conflict of interests, most of it, we suspect, is a product of the fears of the imagination. Yet imaginary fears can cause real suffering."[10]

Here, Allport describes the 1950s, but it is no great leap of the mind to apply his words to the twenty-first century. Based on the studies and surveys he had found, Allport formulated a solution that was to become known as the contact hypothesis. Allport came to the conclusion that yes, the mechanism observed with the soldiers and the students applies generally.

Contact between enemies dispels prejudice and, often, creates sympathy. But, Allport warns, there is one type of contact that has the opposite effect and actually makes matters worse: casual contact that is so superficial that it merely awakens a prejudice but doesn't allow it to be addressed. The neo-Nazi Sven Krüger would have been a good example.

In Namibia, seeing people sitting in the dust or leaning against their mopeds as he was driving past, Krüger concluded that they were lazy. His prejudice had been awakened. Had he stopped, he might have noticed that many of the women sitting there had spread out small rugs in front of them with mangos or bananas. Had he approached the women, they might have told him that they had picked the fruit in their gardens and were selling them here. Had he spoken to the men leaning against their mopeds, they might have told him that they were taxi drivers waiting for business. Maybe they would have told him something completely different. Who knows? But Krüger didn't give them the opportunity to correct his prejudice. He had only driven past.

Another example: the Hermeses' daughters. Christa and Harald remember that the closer they got to their Serbian neighbors, the more fervently their daughters warned them: "Don't let them take advantage of you!" They didn't want to meet the new neighbors. Their father had always cautioned them against "gypsies," and they took his warning to heart even after he had long changed his own opinion of his neighbors. This Roma family had only entered the lives of the daughters superficially; they were no more than faces that scurried past on the stairs, characters in their parents' stories. It wasn't enough to break down their prejudice. Gordon Allport would have called this kind of contact "superficial."

According to Allport, contact has to be more meaningful. In addition, he specified four conditions that must be met for contact to reduce prejudice: Both parties need to be of equal status (soldiers, neighbors), have a common goal (kill the enemy, good neighborly relations), cooperate on the common goal (lying side by side in a trench, hanging up the laundry together), and finally, the contact needs to have the support of a higher authority (commander, zeitgeist).

Allport published his book during a time of change in America. The civil rights movement was demanding the end of segregation, and supporters looking for a scientific argument to prove their case found one in his contact hypothesis. Step by step, American society opened up for Black people: hotels, restaurants, buses, schools, the army. Once this process was finished, however, Allport's ideas faded from everyday life and were mostly brought up in psychologists' technical discussions.

Among social scientists, Allport inspired hundreds of follow-up studies over the decades. Researchers from dozens of countries tested racial, sexist, political, and religious prejudice. Psychologists carried out experiments in laboratories and in the field (as they call the real world). They applied mathematical methods that had been unknown to Allport. They increased the sample sizes, which rendered the results so meaningful and significant that Allport's discoveries seemed like ornamental anecdotes by comparison. The subject literature grew so diverse and confusing that in 2006, two social psychologists bundled the findings from over five hundred studies on the subject into one formula in a so-called meta-study, a study of studies.[11]

They established that Allport was right. In fact, he was even more right than he had anticipated. Contact works even if none of the four conditions are met. The hypothesis had become a theory, and for the time being, something close to a consensus among social scientists. But apart from the experts, nobody took any notice.

When I stumbled across Allport's work a few years ago, I was electrified, and I still am. Isn't this exactly the remedy that the polarized societies in the West need right now? Surely, the centrifugal forces currently pulling on our society can largely be explained by prejudice. The people most afraid of refugees are frequently the ones who don't know any. In my reporting, I keep meeting people who pass judgment from a distance, who, in Germany, label those who are kind toward refugees as *Umvolkers* (engaged in ethnic replacement) and those who are suspicious of them as neo-Nazis, who declare all Muslims terrorists—all without ever having exchanged a single word with a member of those groups. Don't get me wrong: Some Muslims may be terrorists, some AfD voters may be Nazis, and some journalists may be liars, but thankfully not all of them. In fact, probably very few of them.

When we define an entire group by its most extreme and dangerous members, we lead society into the abyss. In doing so, we create a world clouded by bigotry, populated only by shadowy figures, by terrorists and extremists, by criminals and Nazis, by liars and fraudsters. No wonder so many people are frightened.

It reminds me of medieval maps. In the Middle Ages, cartographers would sometimes draw sea monsters in the middle of the sea. I am picturing a monk in the scriptorium of some monastery, far away from the place he is about to illustrate, lacking any reliable information, dipping his quill into the inkwell, and drawing, with great conviction, enormous snakes, hideous monsters with lion heads, and many-armed creatures with bared teeth. He just assumes the worst. Our political debate is full of sea monsters.

It would have been too much to ask of a medieval monk to leave the scriptorium, travel to the coast, and board a ship before illustrating the sea. Today, thankfully, facing reality is much easier. Talking to a refugee, an AfD voter, a journalist—or anyone you don't like—is easy. In theory. Even so, not everyone does, and what happens when too many people don't is easy to see in many places all over the world.

•••

For an article I was reporting, I went to visit the town of McConnellsburg, Pennsylvania. It has a population of 1,220, two traffic lights, eleven churches, and a well-frequented gun store. The people here are dairy farmers and housewives, truck drivers and auto mechanics—proud workers and aggrieved, unemployed ex-workers. In the 2016 presidential election, 84 percent voted for Trump. A few days after the election, I park my car in front of Johnnie's Diner. An overweight man in a baseball cap sitting at the bar says: "If you're looking for Hillary voters, there aren't any here. And if there were, they wouldn't admit it."

The customers in Johnnie's Diner tell me about the great dangers facing their America: the "illegal immigrants," the liberal city people, and the Blacks. It's odd. I've spent several days in McConnellsburg, and I haven't seen a single Black person. Ninety-seven percent of the inhabitants are White. Visitors from cities are few and far between. There are hardly any undocumented immigrants here. The people in Johnnie's Diner are afraid of people they don't know. They have created monsters inside their heads.

A few days later, in New York, I meet the other side: Americans who quite naturally describe Trump voters—of whom I can hardly find any here—as fascists, racists, or neo-Nazis. When I ask how many Trump voters they know personally, many answer, "None." How is this any different from the people in the diner, apart from the fact that their prejudices are reversed? They too have created monsters in their heads.

At the time, both in New York and in McConnellsburg, I encountered an atmosphere of intimidation, of peer pressure, that only comes from great homogeneity. Studies have shown that Americans moving to a new house are more likely to settle in areas where the residents share their political ideology.[12] The country is segregating itself. Just like in the past, except that the split is no longer predominantly along racial lines (although that still exists too) but between political camps. Just like then, these homogeneous surroundings are breeding grounds for prejudice toward the other.

In a survey, 33 percent of Democrats and 40 percent of Republicans stated that it would "disturb" them if their child married a member of the other political party. In 1960, it was less than 5 percent.[13] On each side, the most politically engaged regard members of the other party not merely as wrong but as "so misguided that they threaten the nation's well-being." In her book *Strangers in Their Own Land*, the sociologist Arlie Russell Hochschild writes: "Our polarization, and the increasing reality that we simply don't know each other, makes it too easy to settle for dislike and contempt."[14] She might as well have added: "Because we settle for dislike and contempt, we no longer get to know each other." The mechanism works both ways: Distance breeds prejudice, and prejudice breeds distance. This escalating spiral has turned America into a society of fear and hatred.

It is tempting to say: America is one thing, but in Europe, in Germany, things aren't so bad. But maybe it would be more accurate to say, "Not yet." After all, we can observe the same phenomena here. Xenophobia is greatest where there are no foreigners. Islamophobia is strongest where there are no Muslims. Hatred of voters of right-wing parties is fiercest where there are only very few of them—in the big cities. It is the absent that trigger fear and hatred. It makes me despair. We know that prejudice is a problem. We know that contact between people who have prejudices toward each other reduces those prejudices. We know that it makes a society more peaceful. And yet we allow this kind of contact to be the exception rather than the rule.

When Sven Krüger returned from Namibia, he retreated into his bubble. His friends, his neighbors, his colleagues—almost all neo-Nazis. When he was released from jail, he did the same. He never saw Thomas Wahnig, Haruendo, or the Palestinian again. Krüger says it's a conscious decision. He avoids contact with those he wants to hate. Closeness leads to understanding, he admits. That's why it was so widespread in German cities, he says, where people go to their Turkish vegetable seller who sells them avocados with a smile. And one day they're asked if they dislike foreigners, he thinks, and then they'll say, "No, I know so many." That's why he keeps his distance, he says, and buys his vegetables from a German shopkeeper, not a Turkish one. To be able to hate, he has to trick his empathy, his humanity.

Society makes it easy for him when it should be doing the opposite. Why not try to intentionally bring about more of those magic moments that Michael Kent, the Hermeses, the farmer Gerold Huber, the White soldiers at Remagen, and even Sven Krüger experienced by accident? Why not organize our societies so that they bring together right and left, rich and poor, queer people and homophobes, young migrant women and old White men to make it grow together where it's currently ripping apart?

In the beginning, I thought that would never work. Who could even enforce something like that, and how? But then, in the course of my work, I came across places, coincidentally at first, where it *had* worked. And then I started consciously looking for them—and found more.

Some of these places are tiny, some are located on distant continents, some in the past. In some of them, a cosmetic political procedure was all it took to arrange contact; in others it was a radical national program that changed hundreds of thousands of lives. In one case, civil servants suffered the consequences, in another it was terrorists. In both cases, it was society who benefited as a whole.

In the following chapters, we will travel to these places. The people there may be very diverse, but they all have one thing in common: They are not content with drawing sea monsters.

They choose the uncomfortable path, the interesting path. And sometimes it is chosen for them. All of them confront their fears and surprise themselves. We will watch their efforts, but first we must make a small but important detour to a Syrian torture chamber.

2

The Hellhole

When the power of contact fails

The terrorists had blindfolded him, tied his hands behind his back, and placed him on the bed of a pickup truck. He could feel the wind on his face and taste the sand in the air. Then they started to sing: "Qul as-salibiiyna: 'amrika qabrak fi suria"—"Tell the crusaders: America, your grave is in Syria."

The American journalist Theo Padnos had arrived in Syria in October 2012 to write about the war that had been raging for a year. Shortly after crossing the Turkish border, he was captured by Islamist fighters. Now he was lying in the back of a pickup truck and thought he was going to die.

When they took off his blindfold, he found himself in a basement cell that was 23 feet by 13 feet, with a wooden door and a small window near the ceiling covered with sandbags, blocking out most of the light. Every few days, the guards would come and beat him with heavy cables. They would shout, "Ta'akul!"—"Eat!" Padnos spoke Arabic and, by overhearing his captors talking, learned that he had fallen into the hands of the Al-Nusra Front, the Syrian branch of Al-Qaeda. He was being held captive in Aleppo, one of the most populous cities in Syria.

Sometimes they would take him to a room that the terrorists called "ghurfat almawt"—the "room of death." In the room, people were hanging from heating pipes under the ceiling, screaming. They would blindfold Padnos, put a tire over his knees, and lock them with a stick. Next, they would flip him over so that he lay facedown on the cold cement, with the bare soles of his feet pointing up. Then they would whip the soles of his feet with cables. Sometimes they would come into his cell and throw his food on the floor. They'd say: "It's dirty in here! Clean the floor with your tongue!"

Just a few miles away, another American was looking through the viewfinder of his camera. Matthew Schrier, a photojournalist, was following to the front line members of the Free Syrian Army, a faction engaged in the Syrian civil war attempting to bring down the government. After three weeks, he had taken pictures that he hoped would make it onto the front pages of the major American newspapers. On his way back to the Turkish border, his taxi was stopped by men shrouded in cloaks, and he was kidnapped. He too was locked in a cold, dark basement cell. Outside, he heard people screaming. He didn't know that Theo Padnos was just a few cells away.

A few days later, the terrorists came to Schrier with a laptop. He gave them his email password and his credit card PINs. They spent $17,000 on computers, tablets, Mercedes parts, and Ray-Ban sunglasses. After three weeks, they picked him up from his cell, led him down the corridor, opened another door, and said "Amriki, Amriki"—"An American, an American." In the dark, Schrier saw somebody sit up with a start, a guy with a matted beard, who reeked.

Padnos's first thoughts were: Now I have a friend. For three months, he hadn't spoken with anyone apart from his torturers. He was glad. That first night, he and Schrier talked for hours.

Our urge to communicate is so strong that prisoners in solitary confinement look forward to seeing their guards even if they are maltreated by them. It would seem to be a stroke of luck that in this Syrian dungeon, a place so hostile, remote, and brutal, these two men met. After weeks of torture, mortal fear, and loneliness, they not only got a fellow prisoner, but a fellow countryman. And not just a countryman, but a journalist. Now they were like-minded companions. Now they would be able to listen to and encourage each other—to give each other hope. Maybe they could even plan their escape together. But soon Padnos and Schrier realized that it wouldn't be that easy.

Every time somebody passed by their door, Padnos flinched. So Schrier tried to make him laugh. He told him a story about when he and his best friend played a prank on their high school teacher by hiding the book that he used to keep notes about the students. The teacher completely lost it, Schrier told Padnos. He called them assholes and broke a pool cue over Schrier's head. That was, in Schrier's experience of telling this story, the moment where people laughed out loud, but Padnos only said that he felt sorry for the teacher. Not only was he badly paid, he had to deal with these screwed-up kids. Schrier replied: "No, you idiot, the teacher is the asshole, don't you get that?"

A few days later, Padnos was picking his teeth with sunflower seeds, as the Arabs do. The quiet tick-tick-ticking noise was annoying Schrier, so he asked Padnos to stop. When Padnos continued, Schrier clenched his fist and shouted that Padnos would find it difficult to clean his teeth if he didn't have any left. After that, they didn't talk for a while.

Padnos had a PhD in comparative literature; he liked reading the Austrian poet Rainer Maria Rilke in the original German, had lived in Paris for many years, and spoke excellent Russian. The only other language Schrier knew was the language of the street. He had been expelled from high school and had spent two months in jail for breaking and entering when he was sixteen. While the teenage Padnos was reading books, Schrier, on the streets of New York, was learning the lesson that if you don't hit back, you'll go down.

In the cell, Schrier had developed a method for killing bugs in the cleanest possible way. He would peel the label off a water bottle, fold it in half, put the bug in the fold, and squeeze. Padnos, however, usually squashed them with his finger on the floor. Once, when Padnos walked through the filth and then over the mattresses, Schrier lost it and punched Padnos in the face.

Sometimes they would play "guess the movie" using a quote, or twenty questions. Schrier could not understand how Padnos had never heard of "Say hello to my little friend." Padnos had never seen *Scarface*; in fact, he had never owned a TV. He didn't know any rappers or characters from TV series, either. But Padnos knew Renaissance artists and poets whom Schrier had never heard of.

In March, after three months of shared hell, the terrorists brought a Moroccan man to their cell, a large guy, maybe two hundred and fifty pounds, a jihadist who had traveled to Syria on his own account and had aroused the suspicion of the Nusra men. He had a gunshot wound on his leg that had never been treated. He had lived in America and spoke good English. Schrier was glad to have someone other than Padnos to talk to. The Moroccan thought the prank story was hilarious. They talked about movies and even shared a mattress. Padnos tried to keep out of it.

On June 9, 2013, Schrier turned thirty-five. The Moroccan wished him a happy birthday; Padnos did not. A few weeks later, the terrorists transferred them to a different prison, located in the old vehicle registration center in Aleppo. Their new cell was also in the basement. Just below the ceiling, about seven feet up, there were two broken windows to the courtyard. They were barred, but the brickwork was crumbly, and a few of the pencil-thin bars were loose. There was a chance of escape, but there was no way the Moroccan would fit through. One day, the guards came for their fellow prisoner. He was barely gone before Schrier asked Padnos, "Do you think we'd fit through?"

Over the course of three days, Padnos went down on all fours while Schrier stood on his back and tried to pry the bars out of the crumbling mortar. Some were anchored down, but only at one end. He bent them outward. They used T-shirts to fashion a ladder with loops for rungs.

One day in late July, Schrier looked out the window into the courtyard. It was during Ramadan, and the guards had brought them their food early in the morning, when it was still dark. He could see no guards, just the wall, interrupted by a gate, and the road behind, the silence of which seemed to beckon him. Shortly before sunrise, Schrier dismantled the window.

Padnos gave him a leg up, and Schrier stuck his head out of the window, followed by his shoulders. He made his body as small as he could, but he got stuck. Padnos pushed from below. Schrier struggled away, twisting his torso this way and that until he finally made it through. The rusty bars had scratched bloody marks into his chest. Outside, he crouched down; above him was a second window. It was open, and a light was on in the room behind it. That's where the terrorists must be, he thought.

Padnos passed him his sneakers, a T-shirt, and his cap from inside the cell before stepping onto the first rung of the T-shirt ladder. He reached his hand through the window, and Schrier grabbed it and pulled. But Padnos got stuck too. Schrier pulled from the outside—but only half-heartedly, Padnos thought—to no avail.

I spend many hours listening to both men tell their stories, Theo Padnos in Paris and Matthew Schrier in New York. Those few minutes on that fateful July morning are the only sequence where their versions of the events fundamentally contradict each other. Schrier says he tried to pull Padnos out for a whole minute, but Padnos had extended only one arm, and that hadn't been enough. So, he says, he whispered to Padnos, "Go back inside, take off your shirt, and come out with both your arms stretched out." Padnos, he adds, already bleeding heavily, did exactly that. Schrier says he set his leg against the wall and pulled—for how long, he can't remember, maybe three or four minutes. At some point, he says, he told Padnos he'd go and get help, and Padnos said "Okay." He insists that he would not have been able to leave without his okay.

Padnos, on the other hand, says that Schrier did not set his feet against the wall, which is why Schrier didn't have the strength to pull Padnos out. He says Schrier grabbed him by only one arm and only by the side. That wasn't enough, he says. Then, he continues, Schrier said: "You're not gonna make it, man."

Padnos says he replied: "I will, nearly there, just a bit more." But then Schrier said he would get help, Padnos recalls, and that's when he gave up and mumbled "Okay." The whole affair, he says, lasted less than a minute. Then, Padnos says, Schrier left, and he stayed behind, alone in the cell.

To better understand the discrepancy between their accounts, I spoke to Mechthild Wenk-Ansohn, a psychotherapist based in Berlin who has worked for years with traumatized war victims. When I tell her about Schrier's and Padnos's reports, she explains: "The mind is not a video camera. Each time we retell an experience, it gets reconstructed." In life-and-death situations, she adds, our sense of time is particularly affected: "We may experience brief moments as an eternity, or there may be gaps in our perception." So, if the two men's recollections differ, it doesn't necessarily mean that one of them is lying. It may just be that they experienced the situation differently. But for Schrier and Padnos, the details in which their reports diverge are of existential importance. To them, the question is whether Matthew Schrier did everything he could, or if he abandoned Theo Padnos.

Having left Padnos behind, Schrier wandered through the deserted streets for half an hour. At dawn, some locals led him to the Free Syrian Army. He told the soldiers where he'd come from and that Padnos was still there. Could they rescue him, he asked? No, they said, claiming it was too dangerous and that it was a miracle Schrier had managed to escape at all. The next day, they drove him to the Turkish border, past the spot where he had been kidnapped. Four armed fighters sat in the car with him. At the checkpoints, they pointed their AK-47s out of the window and were waved through. A few days later, Schrier landed in New York.

Finding Padnos alone the evening that Schrier escaped, the guards beat him to within an inch of his life. For several days he wasn't given anything to eat. He was hoping that President Obama would send the CIA or a platoon of Navy SEALS to rescue him; he assumed that Schrier had explained exactly where he was. But two weeks later, the terrorists moved Padnos to the desert and locked him up in a tiny, boiling-hot cell. Months passed. Eventually he was given more freedom to walk around; in the desert, he couldn't escape anyway. Then one day, one of the guards said to him: "They'll let you go soon. We need the money." In August 2014, more than a year after Schrier's escape and after Padnos had spent more than twenty-two months in captivity, his captors took him to the Israeli border and set him free. The Qatari government had paid the ransom.

When asked about his time in captivity, Theo Padnos is less angry at the terrorists than at Matthew Schrier. Those seven months in his company, he says, were worse than the torture, the mortal fear, or the loneliness.

It's odd, isn't it? The meeting between Padnos and Schrier sounds like it's straight out of Gordon Allport's textbook. They were as close as two people can be, for seven months, twenty-four hours a day. They got to know each other better than almost anybody else in their lives. Their encounter even fulfilled the conditions Allport had formulated half a century earlier. As prisoners, the two men were of equal status. They had a common goal that could not have been more fundamental, meaningful, or unifying: to survive and to escape. And in order to achieve it, they had to cooperate. One man had to endure kneeling on all fours for days to support the other standing on his back.

According to Allport's rules, they should have developed an inseparable bond. They should have gotten along famously, even more so than the Black and the White soldiers at Remagen, or the Hermeses and "their Serbs." Yet, it looks as if the exact opposite had occurred. The longer the two men spent in each other's company, the more they hated each other. Does that not disprove Allport's contact hypothesis?

It does only at first glance. In fact, the episode is a prime example of the hypothesis at work. What is more, it illustrates a key aspect that is sometimes overlooked. Closeness does not automatically lead to sympathy. Closeness breaks down stereotypes, but not just negative ones—positive ones too.

Just the way the Hermeses decided that their neighbors must be enemies based on their origin and looks, Padnos and Schrier both decided by the other's origin and looks that he must be a friend. How could it not be so, with the other also being a White, American journalist? Just like the Hermeses, Padnos and Schrier were wrong. They had been taken in by their stereotypes.

Everyday life in the cell had brutally ripped the mask of stereotype off the other man's face, and the person exposed behind it was very different from what the other had expected. With the two men divested of all cultural attributions and reduced to their personalities, a new reality took hold in the cell: Suddenly, the New York street kid and the Moroccan jihadist had more in common than the two Americans who were nothing more than phenotypical twins.

It was the same as with the twenty-seven high school students from Ohio that Allport had written about. After the trip, twenty of them had indeed become more popular, but at the same time four of them had become less popular. Just as the twenty had been prejudged unfavorably, these four had been prejudged favorably. Just like Padnos and Schrier.

It is important to get this right: Contact does not always result in sympathy. More contact in society, therefore, does not translate into a shiny-happy-people world; unfortunately, it's not that simple. Sometimes, contact can cause new conflicts, as it did for Padnos and Schrier. Their world would have been, surprisingly, less painful if circumstances hadn't brought them together and if they had been allowed to maintain their positive stereotypes of each other.

Consequently, a society institutionalizing intergroup contact would still have to put up with conflicts, but only those based on actual differences, not imagined ones. "Actual or imagined," one might say, "it's all the same; conflict is conflict; hate is hate." But that's not true. Conflicts based on actual differences are markedly rarer.

Mechthild Wenk-Ansohn says that in twenty-one years of working with people affected by war, she has never seen a dynamic like the one between Padnos and Schrier. Usually, prisoners in extreme situations stick together, she says, even across deep ideological divides; Kurds would help Turks, and Sunnis would help Shiites. The school class from Ohio is no different. Twenty students became more popular, only four less so. More conflicts disappeared than new ones arose. Overall, the result was positive. Theo Padnos and Matthew Schrier are the exception.

Fact-based conflicts have one fundamental advantage: They are directed against an individual—against the neighbor who hasn't cut their grass, against the spouse who's having an affair, or against the prisoner who cleans his teeth too noisily. They're not directed against all neighbors, or against all spouses, or against fellow prisoners, per se. Fact-based conflicts home in on the small things, the individual.

Prejudice-based conflicts are different: Arabs can't do democracy, men can't be faithful, Jews can't be trusted—no matter what the prejudice, whether it's racism, sexism, or anti-Semitism, the conflict will focus on the big things, the generalizations. They expand outward like supernovas and affect many innocent bystanders in the process. A contact-rich society, therefore, would not be conflict-free, but on the whole, it would be calmer, more peaceful, and more convivial.

The question is, how can something that worked for twenty-seven children on a school trip be applied to 80 million Germans or 330 million Americans? After all, we can't send entire nations on school trips.

If an American wanted to get in contact with each of their fellow citizens and, say, talk to them for an hour, they'd have to talk nonstop for nearly forty thousand years.

Now, you may say, you don't have to speak with *everyone*. Harald Hermes met only one Roma family. If he were to meet a man from Bavaria or a woman from Lower Saxony, a Swabian, a Berliner, a queer person, a Muslim, a Jew, a street cleaner, an investment banker, a cat lover, or a dog hater—representatives of groups who would rectify his prejudices toward that group— would his prejudices not just disappear one by one?

That's the problem; they wouldn't necessarily. Most people are steadfast in their views, and they like to be right. Harald Hermes is no exception.

• • •

During one long interview in their living room, Christa and Harald Hermes emphasized how their hearts overflowed with love for "their Serbs" and how they can't understand the other neighbors who stick to their prejudice even though they, the Hermeses, keep telling them how wrong they are. Harald Hermes, this no-nonsense kind of man, speaks so tenderly of his Roma neighbors that I am dumbfounded by his response to my final question. At the end of our conversation, I ask him how much his lifelong views of the Roma people have changed. He looks at me in surprise and says his views of the Roma haven't changed at all. He just doesn't call them gypsies anymore.

Harald Hermes says he still thinks that the Roma are dangerous swindlers. I question if that isn't contrary to his experience with his neighbors, but he says, no, they were just lucky that "their Serbs" had been the *right* kind of Roma. So, the Hermeses did change their views, but only concerning the six people who had moved into the flat above, not the entire group that their neighbors belong to.

Social psychologists observe this train of thought frequently. Because people don't like to give up their prejudices, they tend to declare any information inconsistent with their beliefs to be an exception. Harald still doesn't like Roma, but "their Serbs" are wonderful. Sven Krüger, a neo-Nazi, still doesn't like Africans, but his hunting partner Haruendo is a great guy. Their worldview may have become more nuanced, but on the whole it remains false.

Often, our friends share not only our opinions but also our prejudices. That's how we form a bond. Let's take Sven Krüger, for example. His neighbors are neo-Nazis, his friends are neo-Nazis, and even the employees at his demolition business are neo-Nazis. His social life is based on racist prejudices. Were he to suddenly claim that Africans weren't inferior after all, he would have to constantly justify himself. His neighbors, friends, and colleagues might call him crazy. Where there was comfortable unity there would be conflict. Discarding one's prejudices makes life more complicated.

If meeting one member of a stereotyped group isn't enough to change a person's opinion about that group as a whole, and if one person can't meet with all his fellow human beings, what else can be done? How could Harald Hermes and Sven Krüger be made to abandon their prejudices after all? They would have to meet so many members of a group that they could no longer explain them away as exceptions. Like Gerold Huber, for example, who had two thousand refugees move into the farm next door. Or if they could meet just one person, it would have to be a very special one who is able to do what the Roma family and Haruendo weren't able to. There will be examples for both of these situations in the following chapters.

But there is a third option, a kind of institutionalized contact that we don't have to reinvent, just repair. It has been around for a long time, but it doesn't seem to work properly. Very early on, mass societies created institutions that were intended to remove the need for the Harald Hermeses of this world to travel to Bavaria, to Swabia, to Saxony, or to Berlin; institutions whose job it is to bring these places and their people to him: the media.

3

The Race

Why the media are making it worse

Cologne cathedral is a breathtaking monument of medieval architecture and one of Europe's finest churches. It's also located in the very center of Cologne and has a huge plaza next to it. On New Year's Eve 2015, about a thousand people gathered there, presumably to celebrate the arrival of the new year. But the story that emerged out of that gathering and gripped Germany's attention for weeks afterward was not one of peaceful celebration but of sexual violence. Many of the people who had gathered next to the cathedral that night were young men from North Africa, many of whom had immigrated to Germany just a few months earlier. That night some of them assaulted women in the crowd. Hundreds of cases were filed with German police over the next few days. It was a huge story.

Barely two months later, three girls, fifteen, sixteen, and seventeen years old, were strolling through the Sophienhof shopping mall in Kiel, the capital city of the state of Schleswig-Holstein in northern Germany. As the teenagers were sitting down at an Italian fast-food restaurant, several immigrant men start harassing them. They made lewd gestures, filmed the girls with their smartphones, and shared the clips on social media. This attracted another twenty to thirty men, all migrants, who joined the others in harassing the girls. The girls ran away but were pursued by the men. At last, alerted by a passerby, the police arrived and arrested a number of the offenders.

It's Thursday evening, 7:51 PM. Like any other decent newspaper, the local paper *Kieler Nachrichten* employs reporters who have their ears to the ground. The next morning, Friday, 10:15 AM, the paper publishes an article on its website titled MASS MOLESTATION OF GIRLS IN KIEL.

A few minutes later, the German news agency dpa reports the story.

At 2:20 PM, the tabloid *Bild* posts on its website: KIEL MOB BEGAN AT THIS PIZZA STALL.

At 3:45 PM, disturbed by the reports, Stefan Studt, secretary of the interior for Schleswig-Holstein, steps in front of a forest of microphones and declares, "Incidents of this kind are unacceptable."

At 4:21 PM, a headline appears on the website of the newsmagazine *Der Spiegel*: GROUP OF MEN HARASS GIRLS IN SHOPPING MALL.

At 5:40 PM, the British tabloid *Daily Mail* reports on the events in Kiel.

At 5:50 PM, @achimasche tweets, "This isn't my country anymore! #sophienhof"

At 7:01 PM, Wolfgang Kubicki, deputy leader of the liberal Free Democratic Party (FDP), demands a forceful response from the state and declares, "Young men who live penned up for a long time and with little to do tend to turn to sexual harassment."

At 7:49 PM, @nohmixx tweets, "Just close the borders and kick the criminal migrants out. #Merkel #Sophienhof"

At 7:51 PM, *Stern* posts: UP TO THIRTY MEN CHASE GIRLS THROUGH MALL.

At 8:08 PM, prime-time news anchor Judith Rakers tells millions of German viewers, "In a shopping mall in Kiel, three young women have been harassed by several migrant men."

At 12:12 AM, @klingeldraht tweets, "Isn't it time these low-lifes are interned in camps, for the protection of the local population? #sophienhof"

At 2:13 AM, Fox News picks up the story: "Group of foreign men harasses girls in Germany."

At lightning speed, the Sophienhof incident makes headlines across Germany and the world, making its way into the minds of millions of people. I also read the story, and like many others I am shocked. A few weeks later, I traveled to Kiel to look into the background of the story. Afterward, I am still shocked, although no longer by what happened at the Sophienhof mall but by what went on in countless editorial offices around the world.

Because it turned out that the story wasn't true.

This is what really happened: As the three girls were sitting at the table, two Afghan refugees, both seventeen years old, walked past, stopped, and smiled over at the girls. The girls thought that was inappropriate. The boys said something in a foreign language. The girls asked the boys to leave them alone. One of the boys blew kisses at them. This continued back and forth for some time. Other men who were passing by or were sitting at other tables in the restaurant began to watch what was going on but didn't bother the girls. Two of the girls then went outside to smoke. They were not followed. When they returned and rejoined their friend, they found the two Afghans still there, looking over at them occasionally and laughing provocatively. A bystander called the police.

There had been no chases or pursuits, no filming or sharing on social media. There had been no mob, just two unruly Afghan teenagers who had crossed the line. The girls had exaggerated the events in their report to the police.

They didn't lie, one of them says when I ask her about it later. But she admits that some of the accusations they put on record in their witness statements were wrong. Comparable situations likely occur on school playgrounds day in and day out. In this case, though, the teenagers' inaccurate version of events reached millions of people, bypassing the journalistic filter designed precisely to prevent that outcome. How did that happen?

Just like physicians (who keep the people in a society healthy) and police officers (who keep them safe), journalists provide a public service. They inform the people about what is happening in their country. It is not limited to what laws have been passed or which football team wins the championship; it is much more fundamental than that. For example, I have never been to Dover in England; nevertheless, I have an image of its white cliffs in my head. I have not been to a gathering of coal miners in a bar, but I can hear their bawdy, beer-soaked jokes. I must have seen a TV documentary. You could probably tell me what you think of Canadians, or what you find irritating about Texas, or if you'd be interested in a trip to Italy, even if you've never been there. Maybe a friend has told you about it, or you've seen photos on Instagram. But often those images form in your head while you're consuming the news, watching TV, listening to the radio, or reading a magazine article. In other words, these images are created by journalists.

Therein lies the journalists' job: to ensure that the pictures they paint are as consistent with reality and as factual as possible. But there's a problem. Journalists are human beings, and by nature, human beings think in categories, in stereotypes. This mode of thinking is embedded deep in our brains. In the jungle, we're alarmed by anything long and thin. Within milliseconds, our brain warns us: long and thin equals snake, equals danger. In a new city, if we're looking for a bar, we wouldn't ask an old lady for directions; we'd ask a young person, reasoning that old ladies don't frequent bars, but young people do.

On the one hand, this is a good thing. Over the course of human history, being alarmed in the jungle has saved many lives. Shunning old ladies has (probably) saved many partygoers a lot of time. But what if the long and thin object wasn't a snake but merely a harmless piece of vine? What if the old lady knew every bar in the neighborhood but the young person not a single one? What if our stereotypes and preconceptions led us to draw the wrong conclusion? In a new city, it would have little significance. In the jungle, however, it's better to be alarmed once too often than be killed. If that young person doesn't happen to know any bars, we'll just ask another.

In other areas of life, our mind works the same way: Pink equals girl, blue equals boy, bald head equals Nazi. Here, errors of judgment are no longer quite so harmless. How does the mother of a newborn girl feel when we talk about her baby as "he/him" just because she's dressed in blue? What about the left-leaning man with a bald head?

Of course, it would be nice if everyone checked their preconceptions at the door before meeting others to avoid such misunderstandings, but that would be asking a lot. We journalists, however, have no choice. When we start our jobs, we are taught to report out our stories before going public. Reporting usually means contact. Put simply, we talk to the people we write about, asking them who they are or what they think. On behalf of our readers, listeners, and viewers, we destroy our own prejudices.

For example, a few years ago I interviewed a man who freezes people after they die because they hope that, in the future, scientists will be able to bring them back to life. His clients pay him $28,000 for the privilege, and, initially, I thought, *the man has found a way to cash in on the human dream of immortality*. But then I saw that he traveled the length and breadth of the country without pay, that he spent his nights on old sagging sofas. He even showed me his bank accounts. I realized it's not about the money for him; he's a believer in the science. Had I not traveled to meet him I would have written a very different article.

For journalists, every objection is progress. Every *although*, every *nevertheless*, every *but* takes us one step closer to the truth. This readjusting of one's own worldview is the core of my profession. But I can only get there by engaging with the subject matter in question.

In my work as a journalist, I picture the reporting process as a ladder. At the beginning, I'm on the bottom rung: I have not had any contact with the person I'm writing about, and my ideas are shaped by stereotypes. Once I take the first step and start emailing the person, things shift a little. When I speak to them on the phone (the second step) and hear their voice and talk to them, reality starts to push my prejudices further back. (Sometimes, of course, the stereotypes are confirmed, and the prejudices become fact.) After I've met with them in person (the third step), ideally over a few days or even weeks, my original prejudice has often crumbled completely. The truth in the deepest sense of the word might remain unobtainable, but the goal must be to get as close to it as possible, to climb the ladder as high as possible. It takes money, patience, energy, and, above all, time.

• • •

It was just before 10 AM on Friday morning, and at the police station in Kiel, Press Officer Oliver Pohl had just finished a TV interview when his cell phone rang. A reporter from the *Kieler Nachrichten* was on the line, asking about the incident with the three girls at the mall.

Earlier that morning, Pohl had read a short report prepared by his fellow policemen who responded to the scene the night before. It was nothing more than a summary of the girls' statement. On the phone, he confirmed what the reporter had heard, saying that was what he knew too. Then he added, Pohl says, that they had not yet had the time to verify the story.

This is what the reporter should have done himself now. He could have tried to find the girls, or some of the alleged perpetrators; reportedly there had been up to thirty of them. Or— and this might have been the easiest thing to do—he could have left his editorial office and walked less than half a mile down to the mall. There, he could have taken the escalator up to level two and talked to eyewitnesses—at the Ciao Bella restaurant, for example. Instead, he quickly cobbled together an article about what he thought he knew and published it. He stopped at the foot of the reporting ladder—why, I don't know. I left the reporter numerous requests for an interview for this book, which went unanswered.

After the article was published on the *Kieler Nachrichten*'s website, the phones at Oliver Pohl's press office didn't stop ringing. Journalists from all over the country wanted to know what was going on. Pohl and his colleagues got nervous. Ultimately, they still didn't know any more than before, but since right-wing populists had been accusing the police of covering up crimes commited by refugees for months, by refugees, the police station was being encouraged to "proactively publicize incidents involving refugees," he tells me. Nobody should accuse them of covering up anything.

Pohl assigned a colleague to answer the phones, and he retreated into a quiet room to write a press release. At 12:41 PM, it was published on the police website. Without any element of doubt, it states that "three young women were molested." A grave mistake, as Pohl admitted later. But it shouldn't have been a very significant one, since very few people read those press releases anyway. The exception was journalists, and their rule book says that a single source, even if it's the police, is not enough to go by.

Like their colleague from the *Kieler Nachrichten*, the journalists reacting to the press release should have done their research. They could have called the restaurant Ciao Bella. Maybe Qendresa Bytyqi, the staff member who had witnessed the episode the night before, would have answered the phone. She probably would have told them—as she told me later—that in her view there hadn't been any molestation or harassment.

But her phone stayed silent. Many reporters just went ahead and published anyway. Some even exaggerated the contents of the press release. The German tabloid *Bild* wrote about a "mob"; *Stern* claimed there had been a "chase"—neither word had been used by Press Officer Oliver Pohl.

A friend of mine who works at a large online newsroom told me that it was normal for her to publish five to seven news reports a day. Often, she said, the sources were agency or press releases like the one from the Kiel police. I asked her how many of those articles involved her picking up the phone to do at least some research.

"Maybe one," she said. And who would she call, I asked.

"Usually a colleague," she replied, "one with more in-depth knowledge on the given subject."

"So that means," I said, "that you barely ever speak with the people you mention in the articles you publish?"

"There's no time for that," she replied.

This is not a problem specific to a single newsroom, and certainly not that of an individual journalist. The rules of the digital world have forced the pace of journalism, where *up to date* has been replaced by *up to the minute*. The competition, the hunt for the scoop, the race for the first push notification often allows for only a modicum of research, and sometimes even that dwindles into a mere plausibility check by the relevant editor or reporter. In the Sophienhof case, this meant, "Can I imagine that these things happened? It hasn't been long since the incident in Cologne, and the country is openly debating criminal refugees. It fits the picture, and the police will know best."

What would have happened if the press release had claimed, "Three girls harassed thirty migrant men" instead of "Thirty migrant men harassed three girls?" I bet every journalist would have stopped and thought, *Hang on, I need to check that, no matter what the police say.* They would have done their research because the message would have conflicted with their stereotypes.

Every day, hundreds of news articles are published without allowing time for direct contact with the person featured in the report. That results in hundreds of articles partly based on stereotypes. Take these three examples from Germany.

In 2015, many major news outlets reported that North African smugglers were cramming refugees onto so-called ghost ships and setting the autopilot for the Italian coast before leaving the vessels. It wasn't true; the crews had always been on board.

In 2016, the media were reporting about extralegal no-go areas in Berlin because an Arab family clan had allegedly attacked the police on Soldiner Strasse. That wasn't true either, which doesn't mean that such extralegal areas don't exist at all.

In 2018, a man wearing a skullcap was attacked with a belt in Berlin, and the media wrote about the "Jewish victim." The man turned out to be an atheist with Palestinian roots.

In all three cases above, the news report fit the prejudice. Smugglers—ruthless. Arab clans—make their own laws. A man wearing a skullcap—must be a Jew. Even if in some cases that may be true, in these instances it was wrong, and all it took to get it right was a visit to the locations in question. Some media outlets later corrected the errors, but the flood of news articles generated by the original report drowned out the clarifications.

Don't get me wrong: Germany produces outstanding journalism every day—sensitive stories, in-depth investigations, brilliant films and radio programs. But the best, the stars, and the prize-winners are one thing; what is important is the average, the sum total. The Sophienhof reports contribute to that total.

If you add up all the reports published by each and every German news outlet every single day, how consistent with reality is the image they generate in people's minds? How would that be in the United States?

Take a stab at answering the four questions below:

1. Out of every hundred people in the United States, how many do you think are Muslim?

2. When asked in a survey, what percentage of people in the United States said that, taking all things together, they are very happy or rather happy?

3. In your opinion, what percentage of girls between the ages of fifteen and nineteen give birth each year?

4. What percentage of the US population do you think are immigrants?

These questions are part of a survey called Perils of Perception conducted by the market research firm Ipsos MORI in 2015, 2016, and 2017 among thirty thousand participants in forty countries.[1] The researchers compared the responses with the actual figures: The greater the difference, the more distorted the people's perception of reality and the more condemning the result for the news media as one of the main influencers (social media would be another one). The greater the difference, the more prejudices slipped through the journalistic filter.

Here are the results. On average, Americans thought that . . .

17 percent of the population are Muslim. In reality, it's 1 percent.

49 percent of the population say that they're happy. In reality, it's 90 percent.

24 percent of teenagers give birth every year. It is in fact just over 2 percent.

33 percent of the population are immigrants. It's 14 percent.

Those numbers are not very encouraging, I think. Let's try another test. How do Americans view not just their own country, but the world?

1. In low-income countries across the world, what share of girls went to school until at least age eleven (before the pandemic)?
   * Around 20 percent
   * Around 40 percent
   * Around 60 percent

2. How did the share of the global population living in extreme poverty change over the last twenty years?
   * Almost doubled
   * Stayed about the same
   * Almost halved

3. What is the global life expectancy?
   * 50 years
   * 60 years
   * 70 years

4. There are currently two billion children from newborn to fifteen years of age in the world today. According to the United Nations, how many will it be in 2100?
    * 4 billion
    * 3 billion
    * 2 billion

5. Worldwide, how many one-year-olds are vaccinated against at least one disease?
    * 20 percent
    * 50 percent
    * 80 percent

6. Worldwide, thirty-year-old men on average have had ten years of education. How many years is it for women of the same age?
    * 9 years
    * 6 years
    * 3 years

7. Worldwide, what percentage of people have access to electricity?
    * 20 percent
    * 50 percent
    * 80 percent

These questions have been taken from the so-called Gapminder test established by the Swedish physician Hans Rosling.[2] In recent years, he has surveyed tens of thousands of people around the world.

The correct answers are:

1. 60 percent

2. Almost halved

3. 70 years

4. 2 billion

5. 80 percent

6. 9 years

7. 80 percent

Did you get some wrong? Or even most of them? Don't worry, you're in good company. Let's look at question 2. Over the last twenty years, the share of the global population living in extreme poverty has fallen by almost half. Rosling considers this to be a revolutionary global development, maybe even the most important one since World War II. How many people in the United States got this question right? Five percent. What about question 5? Eighty percent of all children worldwide are vaccinated. Only 17 percent got it right.

Rosling's questionnaire consists of twelve questions. In 2017, twelve thousand people around the world took the test. Not a single person knew all the answers. One—a man from Sweden—got eleven right. Almost one in six got none of them right. On average, people answered two questions correctly. Two out of twelve; that's not even 17 percent.

Chimpanzees in a zoo would do a better job, Rosling writes, if their keeper were to throw three bananas labeled A, B, and

C into their cage and watch which one they'd pick up first. Obviously, the chimps wouldn't have a clue, but sometimes they'd get it right. After several attempts, the animals would eventually average a hit rate of 33 percent.

We humans perform less well as a species, not just Americans. No matter in which country Rosling did the test, the chimps always won. So Rosling started targeting people who by the very nature of their work would be expected to know quite a bit about the world: scientists, journalists, heads of state and government, entrepreneurs, and even Nobel laureates. Again, the animals carried off the prize.

As a result, Rosling was able to show that we don't happen to misperceive the world because we don't know enough about it, like the chimps. In fact, this misperception is systematic. It is precisely because we think we know a lot that we get it wrong. And we always err on the same side. We see the world in far too negative a light.

We overestimate the global impoverished population and underestimate the education of girls and women. More people have access to electricity and fewer have AIDS than we think. In the United States, we just happen to overlook 140 million happy citizens and invent over four million teenage pregnancies a year. In his remarkable book about these phenomena and their causes, *Factfulness*,[3] Rosling holds the media partly responsible for this negative shift of our perception. One of the reasons that he too identifies is the lack of time.

Rosling describes an episode that occurred in October 1975, when he was a young physician working at a Swedish emergency room. A pilot who had been injured in a plane crash was rushed in on a stretcher. He was wearing a dark green military uniform and a camouflage life jacket. His arms and legs were twitching. Rosling took off the man's life jacket and let it fall to the floor. Just as he was about to cut open the uniform, he noticed blood on the floor. Lots of blood.

He asked the patient where he was hurting, and he replied, "Yahze shisha . . . na adjezhizha zha . . ."—it sounded Russian.

This must be a Russian fighter pilot shot down over Swedish territory, Rosling thought, and concluded that the Soviet Union had started World War III. Rosling was terrified but had to tend to his patient, so he addressed the man in broken Russian, "All is calm, comrade. Swedish hospital." The soldier's eyes widened with panic.

Then the head nurse came over and said to Rosling, "Please step off the life jacket. You're standing on the color cartridge, and it is making the whole floor red." And to the patient she said, in Swedish, "You were in icy water for twenty-three minutes, which is why you are jerking and shivering, and we can't understand what you're saying."

Within seconds, Rosling had misinterpreted some very important facts. The blood was red dye, the Russian was Swedish. The war was peace. The plane had not been shot down but had crashed during a routine flight. Under pressure, Rosling had fallen back on his preconceptions, which are often informed by thoughts of worst-case scenarios, by fear. Just as we take flight at the sight of a vine in the jungle, Rosling had imagined World War III.

The same mechanism had led journalists and police to imagine a sexually motivated migrant mob in Kiel in February 2016. The less time journalists have to report, the more negative their published articles will be as a result.[4]

But having more time isn't everything. Even if we could climb to the top of our research ladder before we publish each story, that in itself would not solve the negativity problem. It is likely that our news reports would be far less biased as a result, but compared to reality, the sum total of all reports would probably still be too negative. We journalists prefer the extreme, the extravagant, and the dazzling; we spurn the moderate, the normal, and the nuanced. As we say in our industry, "If it bleeds, it leads." If there's violence and gore involved, it gets top billing.

Extreme cases are, of course, more interesting, and most journalists, including me, would agree. More important, however, we're not the only ones who think so; our audiences do too. And so do you. Have a look at the images below:

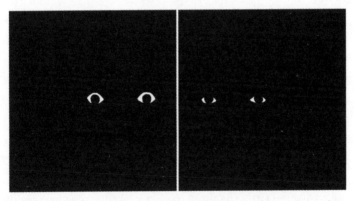

Fig. 1: These images were shown to participants of a study on the responsivity of the human amygdala. See footnote 5.

When you looked at the left image, your pulse quickened even before your brain formulated the thought that these are the eyes of a fearful person.

Scientists showed this image to volunteers connected to a brain scanner.[5] The image was displayed for only seventeen milliseconds, not even long enough for the study participants to realize that they had seen anything at all. But it was enough to activate their amygdala, the area in the brain responsible for detecting danger. Evolution has trained us to recognize the tiniest sign of danger as quickly as possible. When the participants looked at the right image, their pulse did not change. Those eyes are the eyes of a happy person.

In a mass of happy faces, we can immediately spot the angry one, but we take no notice of a smiling face in a mass of angry ones.[6] In newspaper headlines, we register negative words like *war* and *crime* faster than we do positive ones like *love* and *peace*.[7]

It was this negativity radar that saved our prehistoric ancestors from hungry lions and venomous snakes. The mechanism ensured the survival of our species. But in our modern, mass media world it creates an increasing demand for shocking news. Special TV reports on the latest terror attack tend to attract greater audiences; newspapers headlining bad news sell better than those with positive front pages.[8] The more journalists give in to the urge to satisfy this demand (and their own instincts), the more intensely they are stimulating society's amygdala and the more hysterical we become as a result, even when there's no cause.

Harald and Christa Hermes are a good example. During our interview in Hamburg, Harald at one point says quite casually, "Muslims are no good for our country." I reply that this is an unfair generalization. We go back and forth, and I notice he gets more and more nervous by the minute. The next day I listen to the tape, and I understand why. This is, slightly condensed, what was said.

Harald Hermes: The Muslims in Germany are extremists.

Me: How many Muslims do you know in Germany?

Harald (*thinks*): About seven, eight, nine. We had quite a few where I worked.

Me: And they were extremists?

Harald: Nah, they weren't extremists. They tried to integrate.

Me: You say that the Muslims in Germany are extremists although the only Muslims you know personally aren't?

Harald: It's common knowledge.

Me: What does that mean, common knowledge?

Harald: We know from the media.

Christa Hermes: Well, we hear it on TV every day. You can't miss all the negative things there, it makes you frightened of what else lies in store for us.

Harald: You can see all the Islamic countries, there's violence and terror everywhere, there's no country that isn't a dictatorship.

Christa: There's no peace.

Harald: There's no peace among Muslims.

Christa: They sit in their mosques and are constantly being indoctrinated that they have to kill us Christians.

Transcribing the tape, I hear myself pointing out in an unsteady voice that Tunisia, for example, isn't a dictatorship. I could have added that there's no war in Oman or in Iran, or that only very few imams in Germany preach violence. I could have said that I have traveled to many Islamic countries, that it is part of my job to read books about them and that they are much more peaceful than the Hermeses imagine. But I don't say any of that—maybe it's because I can already guess Harald's response: If you journalists know all that, why don't you report on it?

Over the course of three years, the media research institute Media Tenor has evaluated more than nine hundred thousand German news reports featuring Islam in nineteen leading media outlets.[9] More than three out of four reports were about something negative, mostly about terrorism and war. Out of the five million Muslims living in Germany, forty thousand are considered to be Islamists (not to be confused with jihadists or terrorists). That's less than 1 percent, yet they dominate the news.

From their couch, the Hermeses see a truck driving into the crowds at a Berlin Christmas market. They see decapitations in Syria and explosions in Iraq. They see that a Saudi journalist was chopped up by his fellow countrymen. And they hear about an imam in a German mosque calling for holy war. What are they supposed to think if they don't have any dealings with Muslims in their daily lives?

Imagine that an alien had landed his spaceship on the lawn outside the Oval Office a few years ago, met President Trump, and then returned to his home planet. What would he tell his alien friends about the people of planet Earth?

The Hermeses assume that what they see on TV is a true representation of reality, just what we journalists aim for. It should not be necessary to visit and read books about foreign countries in order to know anything about them. Desirable, yes, but not necessary. It should be enough to turn on the TV or open a newspaper.

The authors of the Media Tenor report write, "The increasingly poor media image of Islam of recent years has contributed in no small part to the rise of nationalist movements in Europe and in the USA. Islamophobia is a fundamental part of the increasing fear of foreigners in general and of refugees from the Middle East in particular."[10] In other words, we journalists are feeding the racism we so rightly denounce.

And if you are thinking: *That's ridiculous, it goes without saying that the media only report negative news; everyone knows that it's not representative,* I'd like to introduce you to Daniel Kahneman.

• • •

Born in 1934, Daniel Kahneman is an iconic figure in the social sciences. He welcomes me into his penthouse apartment in Lower Manhattan. Here, from over twenty floors up, Kahneman has an uninterrupted view of the Empire State Building, which he says he doesn't appreciate often enough because he is always staring at this computer screen. He's working on a new book. His last book, *Thinking, Fast and Slow*, was a global bestseller. Kahneman is one of the few scientists who have managed not only to revolutionize their own field, in this case social psychology, but also another field—economics, for which he was awarded the Nobel Prize.

In an experiment in the 1970s, Kahneman and his colleague Amos Tversky asked their students the following question[11]: In which position is the letter *R* more commonly found in the English language? As the first letter of a word? As the third letter of a word? I estimate the ratio to be __:1.

Most students guessed 2:1. They thought that there are twice as many English words that start with the letter R as there are words that have R as the third letter. In reality, it's the exact opposite. Kahneman observed that his students all followed the same method. They searched their minds for words of both variants, like *road* or *car*. As it is easier to look for words by their first letter, they could think of more: *ring, rat, rust, rabbit, run, ROUGH, RULE* . . . They could think of so many that they assumed that their recollection must be representative. But it wasn't, and they were wrong.

In a different experiment, Kahneman read out thirty-nine names: twenty women's names and nineteen men's names. Some were the names of famous people: Elizabeth Taylor, Richard Nixon. The list contained more famous men than women. Kahneman then asked his students whether he had read out more men's or more women's names. Almost all the students answered, "More men's." And they were wrong again. They had remembered the famous people, and most of those had been men.

Then Kahneman modified the experiment: he read out twenty men's and nineteen women's names. This time there were the same number of famous men and women, but the famous women were more famous than the famous men. The students guessed that there had been more women's names—and were wrong again. They had remembered the more famous women.

According to Kahneman, what's going on here is the same principle that makes us drive more slowly after we have seen a

bad car accident, stops us from going into the water after reading about a shark attack, or makes us think twice about going
to a movie theater after a mass shooting. Our behavior is determined by what we remember. What we remember is determined
by how we think about an issue—or about a person. Kahneman
and Tversky call this phenomenon *availability bias*.

Back when the two scientists were doing their experiments,
Americans already believed that tornadoes killed more people
than asthma and that lightning strikes are deadlier than food
poisoning. In reality, asthma kills twenty times more people and
food poisoning fifty-two times more. But those cases never get
reported, while lightning strikes and tornadoes usually make
the news.[12]

When we ask people what they think of Islam, they do what
Kahneman's students did. They search their minds for pointers
and anecdotes that could help them answer the question. And
if they don't know any or many Muslims themselves, then the
memories that emerge will be of media reports. And in America, 78 percent of those are negative.[13]

Let's put ourselves in the shoes of the three girls at the Sophienhof mall. They were just sitting there having their pizza when
two foreigners started hitting on them and wouldn't stop. What
images would pop into the girls' heads first? In the previous
weeks, triggered by the events of that fateful New Year's Eve
in Cologne, the TV channels were full of stories about harassment by refugees. *Wasn't it the same in Cologne?* they may have
asked themselves. They probably panicked, just like one would
panic and run from a "snake" in the jungle even though it's just
a piece of vine.

Current news coverage sometimes achieves the opposite of what it's meant to do, which—to a journalist—is a painful discovery. Instead of reducing prejudices in a society, it reinforces them. Instead of enlightening audiences, it produces false hysteria.

Since journalists aren't getting through to the public by proxy through the news—and not doing the job of ridding a society of its prejudices—it may require more direct contact between its members after all, more moments like the ones experienced by Christa Hermes on the balcony or by Sven Krüger in the prison gym.

In the subsequent chapters of this book, we will look at societies that have managed to bring about such moments intentionally, that have institutionalized contact between individuals who think differently, some by force, some with encouragement. Contact is a tool that can take many forms—and dimensions. Sometimes it's applied with the ruthlessness of a sledgehammer, sometimes with the precision of a scalpel—as happened a few years ago, when the Danish city of Aarhus, an idyllic Scandinavian city discovered an enemy within.

4

The Returnees

How a smile becomes a weapon

The problems began after the boy, who'd like to be known here as Jamal, returned from Mecca. Twenty years old, Jamal was attending a religion class at his high school in the Danish city of Aarhus when one of his female classmates said that Islam was a Stone Age religion that had barbaric and inhumane attitudes toward women. In Mecca, Jamal had walked around the Kaaba together with hundreds of thousands of Muslims. They had come from all over the world: from Egypt and Tunisia, which were soon to experience the Arab Spring; from democracies like the United States and authoritarian countries like China; from Somalia, his old home country, which was still embroiled in war; and from Denmark, his new home country, where he had fled with his family at the age of five. As a child, he had not been interested in religion, but in Mecca he felt for the first time the kind of belonging that a big group of like-minded people can evoke. Suddenly, he says, Islam felt like a second home. And now, here in this classroom, this girl had slighted that feeling.

Jamal jumped up, planted himself in front of the girl, and screamed, "You should be stoned to death for talking like that!" The classroom fell silent. "Islam is a religion of peace and harmony!" Jamal screeched, "It's you guys who fight against Muslims all over the world!"

"That's enough," said the teacher.

That evening, Jamal was out with his friends when his phone rang. He instantly recognized the tone of his father's voice: He was in trouble. Big trouble. Jamal went home and, without a word, sat down on the sofa. "What did I do?"

Plainclothes police officers had come to the house, his father said, and had asked for him, with no reason given. For three hours the father interrogated his son. "What did you do? Did you hit someone? Did you rob someone?"

"No."

"What did you do?"

"I don't know."

As Jamal tells me this story in the summer of 2018, eight years after the event, his voice is so gentle that I find it hard to picture him screeching in the classroom. Jamal recounts the conversations and details almost as if he were watching a movie in his head. He remembers everything so clearly, he says, because what happened that day set in motion a series of events that nearly got him killed and still affect his life today.

That night he lay awake, he remembers. The next morning, ordered by his father, he took a bus to the police station in the city center. Police officers led him to a meeting room on the fourth floor, the department for violent crime. There was a note on the table, he says, with the letters PET on it—the abbreviation for the Danish security and intelligence service. The police deny this but confirm that the other events happened as described by Jamal.

"Are you Muslim?" Jamal remembers the police asking.

"Yes."

"Are you a Sunni?"

"Yes."

"You went to Mecca. Are you planning to blow yourself up?"

"No. Pilgrimage to Mecca is one of the five pillars of Islam."

The previous day, after the religion class, some of his classmates had told their teacher that they were worried Jamal might be a radical. The teacher had gone to the principal, who had called the police. And now, Jamal was sitting across the table from police officers who were asking him questions about his journey to Mecca. Jamal began to panic.

He had seen TV reports about innocent Muslims from Germany and Italy being carried off to secret American jails. "I thought I was going to be next, that I'd be on the next plane to Guantánamo," Jamal says. The police asked him to sign a document. He had no choice, he says. Two officers in blue uniforms, the emblem of the royal crown stitched on their shoulders, drove him back and searched his family home.

Jamal remembers his mother's shock as they watched the police pull open drawers, search closets, and inspect his little brother's computer. Inside, Jamal was boiling with rage. They were humiliating not just him but now his family too. Then they asked for his passwords for his social media accounts; he told them.

Afterward, he slept and ate little. He stopped going to school and missed important exams. Every day, he says, he went for a walk through the woods, alone with his thoughts. *Why are you letting this country treat you like that? This society doesn't want you. Why else would they humiliate you like that?*

Two weeks later, the police called to say that he was in the clear. Jamal wanted to retake his exams, but the principal said that wasn't possible. He either had to repeat the whole year or go to a different school. Jamal told his father, "These people are racists. How can we belong to this country?"

Shortly after that, his mother became sick and died, and Jamal's world lost its last remaining shred of meaning.

At home, his father and siblings cried. So he went back to the woods. The emptiness turned to rage. *The Danish doctors should have saved my mother. The principal is a racist. The police have humiliated me.*

Everywhere, Jamal says, he heard society bellow, "You don't belong to us."

Then one day, he says, there was a moment when he was in the woods and a thought popped into his head: *If you want a terrorist, I'll give you a terrorist.*

A few days later he was praying at the mosque when someone tapped him on the shoulder, an old friend he had gotten to know in Quran school as a kid. "Where have you been all this time?" his friend asked. Jamal broke down and told him everything. The friend said, "Don't worry. You're not alone. Others feel exactly like you do."

His friend took him to an apartment in the suburbs where three young men were waiting. They wore beards and Islamic garments. They embraced him. "Welcome, brother. Have a bite to eat." Two of them were from Somalia like him; the other was from Palestine. One said that the police were after him even though he hadn't done anything wrong. Another said that his sister had been spat at for wearing a headscarf.

Sometimes Jamal would see them at the mosque, but mostly he met them in the apartment. They cooked together and watched YouTube videos; their favorites were by the American imam Anwar al-Awlaki, who was hiding from the US government in the Yemeni mountains. In one clip, taken only a few months earlier, al-Awlaki said, "I lived in the US for twenty-one years. America was my home. However, with the American invasion of Iraq and continued US aggression against Muslims I could not reconcile between living in the US and being a Muslim. And I eventually came to the conclusion that jihad against America is binding upon myself just as it is binding on every other able Muslim."[1]

"I liked him because he had lived in the West," Jamal remembers. "He was talking in a way that we could find ourselves in his speeches." The group began to think about following al-Awlaki's call. "My feeling was, if my people, fellow Muslims, are being attacked, I would grab that AK-47 and fight with them."

In the summer of 2012, the phone rang in the annex of the Aarhus police station. It was answered by Thorleif Link, a police officer with twenty-six years' experience. At the other end of the line, a man was telling him that his son had gone missing.

Link called the boy's school—they hadn't seen him for two weeks. Before long the phone rang again. It was another father. He hadn't seen his son for three days. Aarhus has a population of 336,000; it is the epitome of picture-postcard Denmark. Young people don't go missing here, and now there were two so close together. Then there was a knock on Link's office door: another father.

"It was like a tsunami," Link remembers. The three missing teenagers became five, ten, twelve, twenty-seven, and eventually thirty-six. All were Muslim. Soon Link heard a rumor from the families of the missing teenagers. They suspected that their children had gone to Syria, where a rebellion had started against the Syrian government a year earlier. With every month that passed, Islamist control over the rebellion grew. Syria had become the new Afghanistan, the new Iraq—a magnet for jihadists from all over the world. If what Link had heard was true, that magnet had attracted the teenagers from Aarhus too.

Link was not unprepared. The prevention unit of the Aarhus police force that he worked for had developed a program to counter homegrown terrorism years ago in order to deal with Danish-born terrorists who had become radicalized and turned against their own society. The unit had established contact with Islamic communities and mosques. Link quickly realized that most of the missing teenagers were frequenting the same mosque.

The Grimhøj Mosque is located on the outskirts of town, down the road from a car repair shop and a bar where people gather before taking out their dirt bikes. Here they preach Salafism, a particularly strict interpretation of Sunni Islam. The media picked up on the story and reported that the teenagers had been radicalized and sent to wage jihad. When Link talked to the imam and members of the community at the mosque, however, he realized that many there were just as surprised and shocked as the rest of the population. They told him that the teenagers had regarded the imam as a softie, an old man who had given in to the temptations of the West.

Several parents suggested that their sons may have traveled to Syria to help the refugees, to do good. Link says he didn't believe them. He suspected that all thirty-six of them were being trained as terrorists. Maybe they were learning how to build suicide vests, how to use an AK-47. He also suspected that at least some of them would one day return to Aarhus, the city for whose safety he was responsible. He had a problem.

Many governments would respond to such a threat by intercepting phone calls, interrogating family members, dispatching special agents, or launching drones into the sky. They would try to arrest the potential terrorists, or even kill them. But firstly, this is Denmark—hygge country. And secondly, Link is a police officer in Aarhus. He doesn't have special agents, or drones, or even the authority to tap phone lines.

Then one day he heard a rumor that one of the boys had returned from the war zone, a young man whose father Link had met at the mosque. The problem was that the police had nothing on the boy, no evidence, not even a concrete suspicion, so they were unable to arrest him.

Then the phone in Link's office rang again. The boy's father asked if he could come over to the station with his son.

"Sure, first thing in the morning," Link responded. He was a little worried. Would the boy show up with a backpack full of explosives or be armed with an assault rifle? Then again, Link trusted the father. Who knows, he thought, maybe this boy didn't actually fight. The next day father and son came by. The boy had thin arms, a full head of black hair, and a bullet wound in his shoulder. Link offered them tea and coffee. The boy said he had driven ambulances in Syria and delivered emergency supplies from the Philippines. They had run into an Islamist roadblock, he said, and one of the rebels had fired his gun all over the place. One of the bullets had bounced off the ground and caught him in the shoulder. Link didn't believe him. His gut instinct told him that this was a fighter, but he didn't let it show.

Link tried to tell himself that the question of whether this man had attended a terror camp or was telling the truth was irrelevant. That was for his detective colleagues to find out. His job was to make sure that this young man didn't get up to any mischief here in Aarhus. Link's instinct told him that his best chance of ensuring that was by helping the young man reintegrate into society as smoothly as he could. He sent him to the hospital to have his wound looked at and arranged an appointment with a psychologist.

A few days later, the boy called him. He had a friend, he said, who had been with him in Syria. Could he come over too?

"Sure," said Link. The second boy came. "Tea or coffee?" Again Link wasn't sure how much of the boy's story was true. And again he sensed that the young man was surprised that a police officer, an enemy, was so kind to him, so open, so interested—and, yes, so obliging.

Then the boy with the bullet wound called again. There was another friend, he said, who had been in Syria for a year and didn't dare come home because he'd read on the internet that the Danish people were very angry with guys like him. Link told him to call his friend and tell him that he would be pleased to welcome him. A few days later, the third friend was sitting in Link's office. "Tea? Coffee?" Link looked after him. He felt that these youths were looking for a way out, he tells me, and he wanted to show them that path. In no time at all, word spread among the young men and women that there was this police officer who didn't reject them without a second thought but who put the coffee on and listened to them. Link's phone kept ringing. Many of the youths who had gone to Syria were returning, and all of them wanted to talk to Thorleif Link. It was like a second tsunami, this time in the opposite direction.

Jamal was standing in his kitchen when a call from an unknown number made his cell phone vibrate. "Hi, my name is Thorleif. I work for the police and I have heard about your case. Would you like to have coffee with me?"

At the time Jamal had decided he would soon go to Pakistan. One of his friends was already there. But Jamal had not yet left Aarhus. Now, on the phone, he needed a moment to collect his thoughts. That's how both he and Thorleif Link remember it. Then Jamal shouted, "Fuck off! You people have ruined my life!"

Link replied, "The police have done you wrong, and I am sorry about that." Jamal was speechless. A police officer, a representative of the society that he felt had excluded, humiliated, and provoked him, had just apologized to him.

"Why don't you pop over for coffee sometime," suggested the police officer.

"No," said Jamal.

But the officer insisted, asking him again and again. Eventually Jamal said, "Okay." The police officer had piqued his curiosity. On the bus to the station, Jamal says he felt like a secret agent in a movie. He was planning to spy on his enemy. He would find out what this police officer was up to. Sure, it could be a trap. Maybe they would arrest him, but at least his friends would know. It would be the ultimate proof that they were on the right track.

This time, the receptionist didn't direct him to the fourth floor but to a little annex that housed the Prevention Unit. Jamal was received by a friendly looking man with broad shoulders and a smile on his face. That's what stuck in his mind: the face of the system, it smiled.

"Welcome, Jamal, nice to see you. Tea or coffee?"

Link asked him how he was. Jamal swore. But the officer just kept on talking. He said again that he was sorry for his colleagues' behavior. Jamal thought, *He's only pretending. Police officers are evil. Police officers are the enemy. Police officers don't smile.* "It was as if someone wanted to hug me, and I kept on resisting," Jamal recalls.

"It isn't illegal to go to Pakistan," Jamal said to Link. "No one could stop me."

"That's true," Link replied. They talked for about an hour. The longer their conversation went on, the more plausible it seemed to Jamal that what he deemed impossible might actually be true; the police officer might just be sincere. At the end, Link said, "Before you go to Pakistan, would you do me a favor? Come back one more time. I'd like to introduce you to a Danish Muslim."

A Danish Muslim? That's an oxymoron, Jamal recalls thinking. *Either you're a Muslim or you're a part of the system.* He says he wanted to see the face of the traitor.

When Jamal returned to Link's office a couple of days later, he found a slender young man, maybe thirty years old, and with a Middle Eastern appearance, sitting next to the police officer. Jamal greeted Link, then turned to the man and said, "Assalamu alaikum." He had thought of this as a test. Would the man know the correct response to the Arab greeting?

"Wa'alaikum salaam," the man replied.

The Danish Muslim was Erhan Kilic—and in that moment he was relieved. Kilic had pictured a large, bearded, aggressive man who used his whole body to communicate. That was his image of a radical Islamist. But then this skinny boy walked through the door, his eyes darting nervously around the room, his quiet and hesitant voice greeting him in Arabic.

Kilic had slept badly the previous night. *What have I signed up for?* he wondered. But Link, a man he trusted, had said that the boy, whose mentor Kilic was to become, wasn't dangerous. The three men sat down. Link explained that Erhan was an observant Muslim, originally from Turkey, who had just completed his law degree and was working part-time as a substitute teacher.

Kilic saw a tentative smile creep onto Jamal's face. It was as if Kilic's résumé had impressed him but he didn't want to show it.

Jamal asked him, "Do you know what these people have done to me?"

"No," Kilic replied. "Why don't you tell me?"

Jamal talked loud and fast, and Kilic didn't interrupt him.

Eventually, Jamal's voice got softer, and when he finished, Kilic said, "No doubt you have been treated badly. But the only person you are hurting with your actions is yourself."

Kilic explained that he too had experienced racism but it had made him work even harder. He talked about his family, his house, his forthcoming job as a lawyer—the fulfillment of his dreams. Jamal got the impression that Kilic was a happy man.

"You can go to Pakistan if you like," said Kilic, "but think about it. Everyone's a Muslim there. The muezzin calls everyone to prayer, everyone prays together, everyone fasts during Ramadan. Here in Denmark there are only a few Muslims. There are no muezzins, and only a few people fast during Ramadan. You have to think of everything yourself. Where is it easier being a Muslim?"

"In Pakistan," said Jamal.

"What do you think Allah values more in a Muslim, choosing the easy path or the difficult one?"

"The difficult one," replied Jamal.

Within a few minutes, Erhan had managed to invade Jamal's religious comfort zone and left him at a loss for words. With a few questions Erhan had put Jamal's resolution, which had been rock-solid only a few moments before, in doubt. Link had been keeping silent behind his desk, but now he said that he had work to do and suggested that the two men exchange phone numbers.

A few days later, Kilic arrived at the city center café where he'd suggested they meet. Jamal was waiting outside. He asked Kilic to put his arms out like at airport security, then patted him down for microphones and cameras. They went inside. Jamal noticed that he and Kilic were the only customers with black hair.

When Jamal went out in those days, he met his friends in shawarma bars, of which there were many near his home. There, they would drink tea and eat *dürüm*. There, he knew the ropes. He had never been to a place like this, in the city center, where people were drinking wine and eating White-people food, which neither he nor his friends and family could afford.

What to do with my jacket? He thought. He watched Kilic and, like him, put it on the chair next to him. *What to eat in a place like this?* He ordered the same as Kilic, waffles with chocolate. *Can I eat that with my fingers?* He did what Kilic did and used a knife and fork.

Jamal pointed into the room and asked, "Are you one of them or one of us?"

"I am myself," Kilic replied.

For two, maybe three hours, they talked mostly about Islam, about the religion that connected and separated them. Then, they went for a walk along the harbor. They met two, three times a week, in cafés, in restaurants, or at the movies. They discussed Islam, Denmark, and the action movies that Jamal picked for them to watch. Often, Jamal would return to his friends and say, "Give me an argument, something to hold against his. I am losing these debates."

"It was about six months before I unclenched my fist," Jamal recalls. He began to see nuances where before there had only been black and white. *So maybe my principal was a racist, but that didn't mean that society as a whole was racist. Yes, the police had done me wrong at the time, but that didn't mean that they had done it out of malice, or even that all police officers were like that. Yes, Danish Muslims did exist—Erhan, for example.* After a while, their conversations turned to different topics.

Kilic and Jamal started talking more about school, which Jamal had again started to attend. They also talked about what he would do afterward. Jamal was seeing less of his friends from the suburb now. Once he bumped into one of them on the street, and his friend said, "Don't forget about us, brother." Soon after that, his friend went to Syria and Jamal started a degree in finance. Later, he heard that his friend had been killed when the Islamic State seized northern Syria.

During Denmark's next election, Jamal, now twenty-five years old, volunteered to count votes at the city hall. He assisted the very state that he had hated so fiercely. He got married and graduated. It wasn't long before Link called him and asked if he would like to become a mentor himself, if he would do for another boy what Kilic had done for him. "Of course," said Jamal. He started meeting with a seventeen-year-old boy whose disillusionment, stubbornness, and societal rage remind him of his younger self. Jamal told him, "Don't take a position when you are angry. People always make false conclusions when they are angry because they don't think straight. Families have been broken, mothers crying for their children dying in Syria. If you want to see your family suffer, then go ahead. But if you care about your family, please stay."

Sometimes he told the boy about himself, about how incredibly lucky he was—that he would likely have been killed, and that he would possibly have killed others, had he continued on his original path. And, Jamal told him, "Whenever your phone rings, pick it up."

• • •

Let's imagine an Islamist who has been on the receiving end of the "global war on terror." Maybe he was killed, say, by an American drone. Or maybe he was tortured, in Guantánamo or Abu Ghraib in Iraq. If he is ever released, what is he likely to talk about for the rest of his life? Probably the brutality of the American soldiers, about the human rights hypocrisy, and about his pain.

Let's now imagine this Islamist's family, close friends, and acquaintances. What will those people talk about? Even if the man was a terrorist, to them he would be, above all, a son, a father, a friend, or a teammate. If they weren't anti-American before, they most likely will be now.

And how much worse would the effect be if innocent people are involved? What does the Pakistani goatherd think, whose family died when a misguided bomb struck a wedding party instead of a gathering of terrorists? Or what about the mother of the man who had live wires attached to his body because his neighbor had informed against him to settle an old score? Or what about the market vendor in Baghdad whose district was quiet before the American invasion but was constantly shaking with explosions afterward?

Every blow in the Amercian war on terror resembles a stone thrown into a pond. It sends ripples in all directions, ripples of hatred, of rage, and of thirst for revenge, nurturing new terrorists all the time.

Let us now imagine an Islamist who has been at the receiving end of Thorleif Link's anti-terror strategy—Jamal, for example.

What will he talk about for the rest of his life? Probably of the humanity shown to him by Denmark, of his gratitude.

Now let's also imagine this man's family, his friends and acquaintances. Jamal's father is not angry at Denmark but grateful to have his son back, grateful that he was able to dance at his son's wedding and celebrate his graduation from college. It is likely that these people will feel more connected to Denmark than before. That is certainly the case with Jamal's family. A blow in the Danish war on terror also resembles a stone thrown into a pond. It too sends out ripples in all directions: ripples of gratitude and of sympathy. Instead of nurturing more terrorists, it leaves more loyal citizens in its wake.

In 2018, researchers from Brown University conducted one of the most extensive studies ever on the American war on terror, called *Costs of War*.[2] They calculated that the federal price tag for the US response to 9/11, the wars in Afghanistan and Iraq, the endeavors by the CIA, the secret prisons, the drone war, actions taken in seventy-six countries in all, was at least eight trillion dollars.[3] With that kind of money, the federal government could have rebuilt the Empire State Building ten times.

And what is there to show for it? Today, there are four times as many Sunni jihadists in the world as there were before 9/11.[4] It is difficult to prove a correlation let alone a causality between the two, but a 2018 study by The Soufan Center in New York City, a research institute specializing in security policy, concludes that after seventeen years of fighting terror, "the results are mixed at best." The analysts write, "The good news is that there has not been an attack anywhere near the scale of 9/11 in the US since that day, a significant achievement. The bad news is that the ideology that leads someone to fly a plane into a building or drive a car into a crowded sidewalk seems to have metastasized in the nearly two decades since the 'GWOT' [global war on terror] was first announced."[5]

Now that the jihadist hype in Syria has abated and the Islamic State has lost its ground, no more youths from Aarhus have left for Syria. And like the researchers from Brown University, Thorleif Link has done his own calculations. Thirty-six teenagers from his city traveled to Syria; twenty have returned and are now living normal lives as members of Danish society. Most of them have ordinary jobs and are trying to put distance between their current lives and what they consider to be the sins of their youth. That's what Link told me when I last spoke to him, in 2019. Apart from Jamal, none of them wanted to be interviewed. Ten of the youths died in the war; six remained in Syria or Iraq.

Dozens of Islamists who had intended to go but had not yet left, like Jamal, have also been reintegrated successfully. Of the youths who participated in the police prevention program, only one has died. Despite numerous conversations with a mentor, the boy traveled to Syria, where he was killed.

Link now attends international conferences and gives speeches about his approach. His audiences often include police officers, intelligence officials, and politicians. Many of them shake their heads in disbelief during his talks. "These people are terrorists. How can you talk to them?" they ask. To which Link replies, "Why not? It works."

• • •

In his book *Mindwise*, the American social psychologist Nicholas Epley recounts a camping trip with his son.[6] Epley describes how he was getting the campfire going while his son was whittling a branch with his pocketknife. The blade slipped and sliced into the boy's hand. Standing twenty feet away, with his back turned, Epley had not seen the accident, but on hearing his son cry out, he spun around and realized in that instant what had happened. How was that possible?

Epley doesn't have any superpowers, just a normal human brain. Before his body had turned around fully, his eyes had already found his son's eyes and followed their downward gaze, toward the palm of his hand—not to the wrist, the thumb, or the index finger, but the palm. Epley writes that he couldn't measure the angle of a roof even if he "had an hour and a handful of protractors," but in this situation his brain could sense the angle of his son's eyes down to a decimal point within a split second.

Immediately, Epley winced as if he had cut his own hand. His body experienced the boy's pain. That is no superpower either, but perfectly normal. Under certain circumstances, our bodies synchronize with other people's bodies. Have you tried not to smile back when someone smiles at you, not wave back when someone waves at you, not yawn when someone yawns next to you, or even to sit still when thousands are dancing around you at a concert? Close your eyes and imagine such a situation. I bet the mere thought will make you feel uneasy.

This even goes so far, writes Epley, that when he attends one of his son's soccer matches, he has to keep a free space on the sideline of the field to allow for empathy kicks. When a player on his son's team is fouled, he feels the pain too. It's called limbic resonance and is rooted deep inside our biology.

In the womb, for example, babies synchronize their hearbeat to their mother's. When we like a person, we mirror their gestures and postures. Usually we don't even notice that we're doing it. It is driven by so-called mirror neurons, nerve cells in the brain, which were first described in macaques, a type of monkey, in 1992 by the Italian scientist Giacomo Rizzolatti. He noticed that neurons in the animals' brains fired regardless of whether they were reaching for a peanut themselves or saw another animal going for the treat. Later, the same cells were discovered in humans.[7]

In situations like Epley's camping accident, the eyes are first to synchronize, followed by the rest of the body, and finally the mind. In that moment, people feel what the other feels, in this case pain. If the soccer player scores a goal, it's joy. If he misses, it's disappointment. It's called empathy.

Empathy often occurs automatically when people are in proximity to one another. When Rosi points to the bathtub, Christa Hermes feels the old calluses on her own hands at the memory of washing laundry in the bath. When Gerold Huber sees a woman hauling grocery bags along a busy road, he feels her exhaustion. When Sven Krüger watches a fellow prisoner doing bench presses without assistance, he can't help but feel anxious with him.

This mechanism is so powerful that even professional enemies struggle to defy it. Soldiers find it relatively easy to shoot at an enemy at long range. They see only a silhouette, a flag, or a uniform. At close range, it's much harder. They see a face, eyes, the fear in those eyes. They no longer see an enemy; they see a person.

During the American Civil War, soldiers often fought their opponents at a range of thirty yards. Given their marksmanship, a regiment should have killed on average more than five hundred enemies per minute. In fact, it was fewer than two. At the Battle of Wissembourg in 1870, the French killed a mere 404 German soldiers with forty-eight thousand bullets, Dave Grossman, a military psychologist, has calculated.[8] Six years later, American soldiers fired twenty-five thousand bullets at approaching Native Americans, killing ninety-nine. During World War II, surveys have found that only one in five soldiers in close combat pulled the trigger.[9]

The author George Orwell, who fought in the Spanish Civil War, described a similar experience: "A man, presumably carrying a message to an officer, jumped out of the trench and ran along the top of the parapet in full view. He was half-dressed and was holding up his trousers with both hands as he ran. I refrained from shooting at him. . . . I had come here to shoot at 'Fascists,' but a man who is holding up his trousers isn't a 'Fascist,' he is visibly a fellow-creature, similar to yourself, and you don't feel like shooting at him."[10]

This, in a nutshell, is the real power of contact. For many of us, physical proximity activates empathy and tears away any labels we may have attached to the other person from a distance. "Enemy," "Roma," "refugee," "*kanake*"— all these labels lose their meaning until only one is left: human being.

Modern armies train their soldiers to lose their natural empathy because it gets in the way of killing. But the reverse is possible too: to practice empathy where it's lacking—for example, when physical proximity isn't an option.

While researching this book, I spoke with a scientist who occasionally reviews academic articles written by his peers. He is an emotional person, and badly written articles make him irritated. Were he to write his reviews immediately, he says, he'd adopt the wrong tone, so he doesn't. Instead, he types the author's name into Google and looks at their profile page on their university's website. There's usually a photo, so he looks at the photo for a while and then reads the biography. Sometimes it says where his colleague was born, where they went to college, or if they have any children. And suddenly, the author who wrote a bad article becomes a person. The scientist forces himself to have empathy and, as a result, dials down the tone of his review.

Other people use empathy as a tool when it serves them—for example, in job interviews. Some candidates purposely smile a lot because they know that the interviewer's mirror neurons will trigger them to smile too, which will improve their mood. It's the same mechanism but reversed that makes marital disputes escalate so quickly. One partner starts yelling; the other yells back. It's the mirror neurons at work again.

The war on terror works the same way. You hurt someone, they'll hurt you back. You humiliate them, they'll humiliate you back. Link did what candidates do in job interviews. He turned the tables and utilized a fundamental human mechanism in the fight against terror. Thorleif smiled. Jamal smiled back. Never having heard of limbic resonance, Jamal said during our interview, "You can't be angry at someone who's smiling at you."

In the café, Kilic put his jacket on a chair; Jamal did the same. Kilic ordered waffles; Jamal did too. Kilic ate with a knife and fork, and so did Jamal. They synchronized their bodies. Had they been connected to brain scanners at the time, it would likely have shown their mirror neurons firing away. That's what "winning hearts and minds" really looks like. In Iraq, this American strategy failed. In Aarhus, it was a success. The Aarhus police officers managed to defeat the most radical adversaries of their society by targeting them with empathy. But they were not the first to do so. There is another case, one that reveals something that remained hidden in Denmark: Using empathy as a weapon doesn't just change our enemy, it changes us too.

• • •

Günther Dienstfertig was twelve years old when he and his family left the Silesian city of Wrocław that was then part of Germany and now belongs to Poland. They got out just in time before World War II started. His father had been good friends with the former Reich chancellor Heinrich Brüning. Günther's uncle, the physicist Otto Stern, would later receive the Nobel Prize in Physics. They were an affluent family, but the Jewish Dienstfertigs followed their instincts and left their lives in Germany behind to make a brand-new start in America.

Günther Dienstfertig changed his name to John Gunther Dean. At just sixteen, he enrolled at Harvard, and in February 1944, at the age of eighteen, he joined the US Army. His new home country was engaged in war with his old home country, and he wanted to do his bit to defeat the Nazis, who had taken so much from his family.

While still in basic training, he received a phone call from the Pentagon. "Do you speak German?" a voice asked him in German.

"I do," said Dean, with a Silesian accent.

At the end of his training, his unit assembled on the parade ground and saluted. As an officer barked names, one soldier after the other stepped forward and marched off until only one man was left: John Gunther Dean. He was given special orders. While his companions were shipped to France to reinforce the troops that had suffered heavy casualties during the Normandy landings, Dean drove to Alexandria, Virginia, a small town on the outskirts of Washington, DC. From a phone booth outside a drugstore on the corner of Queen and Main streets, he dialed a number he had been given. He was picked up by a car and taken south, out of the city, passing woods on either side of the road.

Before long, his driver turned left at a narrow driveway with a barrier and two guards. Whatever lay behind had been completely hidden from view by the trees. Dean saw military barracks and wide meadows. Dotted between the shady trees were several wooden huts. There was a swimming pool and a tennis court. It looked like some kind of summer camp.

The site was fenced in on three sides; the fourth was bordered by the Potomac. From the bank of the gray, slow-flowing river, Dean could see the top of the Washington Monument piercing the sky a little farther north. What was this place?

In the fall of 2016, Dean receives me in his apartment in the upmarket sixteenth arrondissement in Paris where he lives with his wife, a wealthy French woman. He is ninety years old and

sitting in a gold-embroidered armchair by the window, a wool-
en blanket draped over his legs. On a sideboard, photographs
show him with Richard Nixon, Jimmy Carter, and George H.
W. Bush. Dean was the American ambassador to five countries,
but his career, he says, started in that camp on the Potomac
River. It was so secret, it didn't even have a name. The GIs called
it Eleven Forty-Two, after P.O. Box 1142, where they collected
their mail in a town nearby.

At Eleven Forty-Two, the United States interrogated some of
their most important German prisoners of war, captured at the
front in Europe. Whenever they caught an officer, an SS man,
or a general who had information about troop levels, chains of
command, or the location of German armament factories, they
brought them there: Reinhard Gehlen, for example, major general of the Wehrmacht and chief of Hitler's eastern intelligence
service; or Hasso von Manteuffel, lieutenant general of the
Wehrmacht; or Gustav Hilger, Hitler's leading Russia expert.

In order to interrogate these men, the Americans needed interrogators who spoke German, so they combed through their
own ranks to find some. In North Carolina, an artillery officer
came across a nineteen-year-old GI. "I hear you speak German.
Say something."

The GI started quoting Goethe's famous poem, *Der Erlkönig*
("The Erlking"): *Wer reitet so spät durch Nacht und Wind? Es
ist der Vater mit seinem Kind. . . .*

"Okay, that's enough. I have a job for you." In Texas, they
discovered a young tank driver who would sometimes read the
newspaper to his companions with a thick German accent. In
Virginia, they met John Gunther Dean.

All over the country, the army found young men who didn't just speak a little German, they were fluent. They even spoke Swabian, Saxon, Bavarian, Viennese, and Silesian dialects—simply because they had grown up in those regions. They had one more thing in common: Almost all of them were Jewish. They had escaped from the Nazis and now, in service to the US Army, were eager to take their revenge. But instead of sending them to the European front, the army ordered them to report to Eleven Forty-Two.

The enemy had been brought to them, to this camp, as prisoners. It was as if the US military were putting on the perfect revenge drama. On the idyllic East Coast, peaceful and green and far away from the noise of the war, the balance of power and powerlessness was reversed. The formerly all-powerful Nazis suddenly found themselves at the hands of formerly powerless Jews: 3,451 prisoners, 3,451 opportunities for revenge, for shootings, for beatings, and for torture.

But the young soldiers had been issued a little booklet, small enough to fit into a uniform pocket. Sanford Griffith, an interrogation expert, had laid down the rules for successful questioning. Griffith had interviewed German prisoners during World War I, and his first rule was: Be kind. Don't threaten; don't hit; don't torture, not only because it was in line with international law, but above all, because it worked.

In a lecture based on his booklet, Griffith wrote that people wanted to show how much they knew, and this was especially true for the Germans. They had a "school teacher urge," he claimed. He advised the interviewer to play the dumb student. What Griffith essentially demanded of the young interrogators was to forget all their previously held thoughts about the Nazis:

the racism, the humiliation, and their grief for relatives. It was their job, he wrote, to build positive relationships with the prisoners. "We must cajole, hypnotize, flatter, irritate, charm, and lull the prisoner into talking."

John Gunther Dean had relatives in Europe. It was possible that they had already been killed in one of the concentration camps. And he was supposed to charm these prisoners, flatter and cajole them?

At first, Dean was assigned to the surveillance team. He sat in a windowless room, listening in on the prisoners' conversations on his headphones. The most important prisoners lived two by two in wooden huts, with two bedrooms, a kitchen, and a bathroom. The soldiers called them "mansions." That was part of Griffith's philosophy too. The more comfortable the prisoners, the more likely they were to give up important information, either voluntarily or by talking among themselves. The army had installed huge microphones in the ceilings. When the prisoners were talking, Dean and his companions listened. Sometimes his colleagues would interrogate prisoners while playing chess or Ping-Pong with them. Again, he would be listening in.

Today, the surveillance and interrogation transcripts made by Dean and his colleagues are stored in the National Archives at College Park, Maryland. Reading them, I was surprised by how cooperative most of the German prisoners had been. In private conversations, they praised the kindness of the Americans. They happily drew maps of arms factories and advised their interrogators on the diving depths of German U-boats. One of them disclosed the location of a Hamburg wharf, which was destroyed as a result.

The strategy of flattery and praise worked, but it also produced some surreal scenes: Young Jewish Americans, many of whom still considered themselves Germans, in animated discussion with Wehrmacht officers. On sunny days, they went swimming together in the pool. In the evenings, they went to the camp movie theater.

I interviewed six Eleven Forty-Two veterans and examined two dozen historic interviews with veterans who had already passed away. When asked if they found it difficult to suppress their hatred, their answers were always the same, almost to the letter. Dean and his companions said, "As a soldier, you obey orders." German soldiers had justified their actions with those same words. If the order is to round up Jews, you round up Jews. If the order is to shoot prisoners, you shoot prisoners.

Orders and obedience—the mechanism works both ways. In Germany, it subverted humanity in favor of unimaginable barbarism. At Eleven Forty-Two, it subverted the desire for revenge in favor of unexpected humanity.

What the GIs did at Eleven Forty-Two was very similar to what the Danish police officer Thorleif Link did many decades later. By creating physical proximity to their adversaries, by going swimming and watching movies with them, they enforced contact and generated an atmosphere of empathy. Had brain scanners been available at the time, they would almost certainly have detected active mirror neurons.

This strategy worked so well that the veterans' stories give the impression that the camp's perimeter fence was redundant. In the documents from the National Archives, references to force and violence at Eleven Forty-Two are few and far between. One prisoner died while attempting to flee when he ran into the electric fence. In one instance, GIs led a German prisoner to believe that they were going to gas him by locking his door and blowing dust into the room with a cooling fan. Others tried to get a German U-boat commander to talk by injecting him with cocaine. They tried to get a Japanese soldier drunk. None of it worked.

Those were the exceptions. Typically, the soldiers succeeded where, sixty years later, their successors would fail in Iraq; they won over hearts and minds. But by the final stages of the war, the effect applied the other way around too.

In the spring and summer of 1945, the camp mission changed. It was no longer about winning the war. Now it was about getting the upper hand in the next great conflict that was already looming, the one with the Soviet Union. In this conflict, technology and expertise—areas where Nazi Germany played a leading role—would make all the difference. In a weird way, the imprisoned Nazis had suddenly become potential allies. Consequently, Dean was given a new task.

As a so-called morale officer, his job was to ensure that the high-ranking prisoners wanted for nothing. Gustav Hilger, for example, probably the most important Russia expert in the Third Reich, had been captured in May 1945 near Salzburg. In the famous photograph of the Soviet foreign minister Vyacheslav Molotov and the German foreign minister Joachim von Ribbentrop signing the Nonaggression Pact between Germany and the Soviet Union in 1939, Hilger is standing in the background. He had been a close adviser to Ribbentrop. He had acted as Hitler's interpreter. He knew Stalin; he knew Molotov—and now he was here, with all his knowledge, at Eleven Forty-Two.

Dean would often sit in the sun with Hilger. Sometimes they read the newspaper, and sometimes Dean took him along to Alexandria. There was a café that served great cake. Over coffee, they would discuss the Soviet Union. "Back then, America knew nothing about Russia," Dean remembers, "really, nothing." But now there was this Hilger, who spoke fluent Russian, understood the differences between the various phases of communism, had read Russian writers and historians, and personally knew many intellectuals and politicians because he had lived in the Soviet Union for over forty years. "When Hilger talked, nothing was black and white. Everything was gray," Dean says. "Hilger opened our eyes to Russia."

Dean was impressed by Hilger, who was deeply religious and highly educated and spoke polished German and elegant French, but who didn't speak a word of English. Hilger told him that his son had died at Stalingrad, and to his dismay, Dean realized that he felt pity for him. Without noticing, he had developed sympathy for the man.

In the summer of 1945, so many prisoners were brought to Eleven Forty-Two that they needed more personnel. On June 6, a short, cheeky young man of barely nineteen arrived. Arno Mayer was originally from Luxembourg. He too was Jewish and had fled the Nazis. He had lost relatives in the Holocaust and now, as a morale officer, was expected to be nice to those who were responsible. He had lots to do from the start.

Shortly before, the crew aboard a German U-boat had surrendered in the Atlantic. Packed full of German war technology—V-2 engines, a Messerschmitt 262 in all its parts, and twelve hundred pounds of uranium oxide—*U-234* had been ordered by Hitler himself to sail to Japan. Now the Americans had tugged the boat to the Portsmouth Naval Shipyard in Maine and brought the crew to Eleven Forty-Two. Dean and Mayer were each assigned a new "customer," as they sometimes called their prisoners.

Young Mayer looked after Ulrich Kessler, general of the Luftwaffe, who had been on board *U-234* because he had been appointed military attaché at the German embassy in Tokyo. Kessler had moved into "mansion" T-250, which he was to share with his former subordinate Heinrich Aschenbrenner, an officer of the Luftwaffe. Mayer brought them magazines, whiskey, and sandwiches.

During the day, Kessler and Aschenbrenner played Ping-Pong or enjoyed the sunshine on their veranda. Before they went to bed, they sometimes sang German folk songs. Often, they talked about the war, and when Mayer was present, he would later write down what they'd said. When he wasn't there, someone else was listening in the windowless room. Today, the transcripts fill numerous archive boxes.

"Kessler: [Someone] told me that he went to Mariupol with Panzer Group Kleist, and the locals there greeted them with fruit and flowers and so on, and two days later an SS unit arrived and shot sixty thousand people in three days, with tanks. Because they were Jews, or God knows what.

"Aschenbrenner: Well, Herr Kessler . . .

"K.: Why do you always call me 'Herr Kessler?'

"A.: Well, Herr von Kessler. Well, the thing with the Jews is, it really was the stupidest thing that this Hitler or Himmler . . .

"K.: That was Hitler!

"A.: You think it was Hitler?

"K.: He, and he alone."

Dean's "customer" from *U-234* was one of Hitler's key scientists, an engineer named Heinz Schlicke. He had worked on developing the V-2 rocket with Wernher von Braun. At first, Schlicke refused to cooperate with the Americans. Dean went to work out with him. He took him along to his favorite café. Before long, the German opened up and soon was leaving the camp by car with a soldier, around noon, on a daily basis. He would travel the ten miles or so north to the Pentagon, where he would give talks about radar and infrared technology.

Today Dean says, "I learned something back then. If you want to convert someone to your point of view, you have to talk to them." As with Hilger, Dean built a good relationship with Schlicke. So good was their relationship in fact, Dean says, that he traveled to Germany on an undercover mission to smuggle Schlicke's wife and two children out of the British occupation zone. Dean remembers the family's reunion at a farm in England, and how he watched over the children while the parents celebrated their reunion in the hay barn. About Schlicke, Dean says, "He was a good Nazi."

"Good Nazi"—two words that seem to repel each other like two negatively charged particles. Yet Dean says them out loud with provocative ease. Two words that prove that using empathy as a weapon, as the United States did, changed not only the German prisoners, who became more cooperative as a result, it also changed the American GIs, who, despite all their loathing and hatred, suddenly saw not just monsters before them, but human beings, with all their complexities and contradictions.

Comparable versions of the same story happened hundreds of times at Eleven Forty-Two and also at Fort Strong, a second, very similar camp just outside Boston. The Americans brought sixteen hundred German scientists to their country. Among them were many war criminals, including one SS captain who had been awarded the Iron Cross, the highest medal available in Nazi Germany, by Hitler: the aerospace engineer Wernher von Braun. Upon his arrival in the country, he was received by a young Arno Mayer.

Mayer looked after von Braun the same way he had looked after Kessler. Once, he even took him shopping so that the German could buy his wife some lingerie as a Christmas present, Mayer recalls almost seventy years later during our interview at his Princeton apartment, not far from campus where he taught history for decades. He shows me photographs from the time: Mayer with a boyish smile at Eleven Forty-Two; Mayer sitting at a desk; a group photo of the young Jewish interrogators.

Among the photos spread over the desk are some that were taken in 2007. That year, the veterans who were still alive had gathered where the camp once stood. A stage was erected in the park, and in his speech, an army man drew a line from then to today, from Eleven Forty-Two to Iraq. Mayer was in the audience and so was Dean. When the veterans were called to the stage to receive their honors, Mayer remained in his seat, in protest against American interrogation methods used in Iraq, Afghanistan, and elsewhere. Shortly before, pictures had emerged from Abu Ghraib, the torture prison. Another veteran said on stage, "I am honored, but I'd like to clarify that I do not support the war against Iraq."

When Mayer arrived as a nineteen-year-old at Eleven Forty-Two, he says, he felt like throwing up, because he had to be nice to those guys whom he hated with every fiber of his being. Now, nearing the end of his life, he was proud that he'd been able to do that. "We were humane then. We used common sense and got the information we wanted. I don't understand how that wisdom got lost."

While at the beginning of the twenty-first century, US troops tortured and killed their enemies and—in a spiral of hatred—created even more enemies, Dean and Mayer embraced their enemies and recruited them for the US cause. Schlicke remained in America until his death in 2006. One of his technological inventions is still being used by the US military today to render planes invisible to enemy radar. Wernher von Braun also resettled in the United States. He built the rocket that propelled the Apollo spacecraft to the moon and became friends with John F. Kennedy. He died, in 1977, an American hero.

In hindsight, it is difficult to say who changed whom the most: Did the Americans change the Germans, or vice versa? But maybe that's not important. From the American point of view it was a win either way that enemies became friends who joined their pursuit of the same goal and who, for decades, worked toward the American advantage in the conflict with the Soviet Union. Fundamentally, however, it begs the question of the obvious guilt and the equally obvious impunity of those people who lived the rest of their lives as if they'd committed no crime.

During my interviews with the Eleven Forty-Two veterans, I asked them, "Should men like Wernher von Braun have been punished for the atrocities they committed or enabled during the Third Reich?" Dean said he had no answer to that. But he added that as someone who has spent his whole working life with intelligence officials, he sensed that these men were more useful in a laboratory or a workshop than in a prison cell. Mayer replied that, yes, they should have been punished. He says that the thought that many of them got away with it still keeps him awake at night, especially since kindness and punishment would not have been mutually exclusive. Von Braun, he says, could have been punished and still become a hero.

Seven decades later and four thousand miles farther east, the police in Aarhus use precisely this two-pronged strategy. People found guilty of a crime are sent to prison, where they receive a visit from a mentor like Erhan Kilic. The punishment does not affect the kindness with which the state of Denmark aims to respond to these people. "Because," Thorleif Link says, "one day they will be released."

5

The Lottery

When chance stabilizes democracy

The best time in the otherwise rather unhappy life of Finbarr O'Brien began one day in the fall of 2012. As on every working day, Finbarr drove seventy miles in his mail truck around the small southern Irish town of Macroom. Passing through rolling green hills and crossing narrow stone bridges, he stopped at all 540 mailboxes. Having delivered his letters and parcels for the day, he stopped for coffee on his way home. He was sitting alone at a table when a woman entered the café. He knew her, as he knew almost everyone in the town. O'Brien is a good mailman, the kind of mailman whom people tell where they've hidden the keys in case they're out. O'Brien knows who is ill and with what, where the children are away at college, and which brand of food they're feeding their dog. When the woman entered the café that day, O'Brien already knew that her name was Caroline and that she worked for some sort of opinion research institute. She approached his table. "Finbarr," she said, "how would you like to go to Dublin for one weekend a month for a year to debate a new constitution for Ireland?"

He remembers how he laughed. No, she said, she was being serious. Finbarr had an inkling of what a constitution was, but he had no idea why the country needed a new one.

Caroline said that she had been asked by the government to recruit participants, ordinary Irish people, for a citizens' assembly. No prior knowledge was necessary. It wasn't paid, she explained, but travel expenses would be reimbursed. Was he interested?

Like many Western democracies at the time, Ireland was in the middle of an economic crisis that was becoming political. Many Irish people regarded their elites and the political system as unfair. But while other governments ignored their critics and tried to exclude them from power, Ireland chose to do the opposite. Why not let the people have a say, for a change? What if the people were to take part in the decision-making? And not just trivial matters but important issues like electoral reform, or the abolition of the senate, or even one of the most controversial questions of all, whether to legalize same-sex marriage?

The constitution prohibited same-sex marriage, and the Catholic church, all-powerful in the Republic of Ireland, wanted to keep it that way. But the zeitgeist had moved on; even the conservative government had noticed that. The government knew that the issue needed to be revisited, but if they did it themselves, the outcome was sure to displease someone somewhere: the church, the LGBT+ community, the opposition. A decision made by the people themselves, however, would have unassailable legitimacy.

Referendums were out of the question. Too many people in the country were angry, and nothing mobilizes anger more than a referendum. The Irish government knew this even four years before the Brexit chaos was unleashed in neighboring Britain. So Ireland tried an experiment. They would gather a hundred citizens, selected at random but representing all of Ireland as a group: men and women, old and young, high and low incomes, village and city people. They would discuss all the important issues. No prior knowledge would be required; they would come as citizens, not as experts. They would be given time and information to learn. That way, any emotion would be washed out of the debate like dirt from a gold digger's sieve. What Ireland would be left with would be a balanced, fact-based, representative opinion about the future of the country.

It could go wrong, of course, so a precautionary measure was put in place. The assembly of citizens would only be able to advise and not actually decide on anything. Parliament would not be bound by its decisions. A polling institute was employed to enlist the participants. Just one more change was made: Instead of a hundred citizens, there would be only sixty-six. One third of the seats would now be given to politicians instead.

This is how, a hundred and fifty miles southwest of Dublin, in the small town of Macroom, a woman named Caroline stopped in front of Finbarr O'Brien while he was enjoying his coffee. The mailman, stocky, with a round head and a shy laugh, thought it was a joke—and declined.

"I'm not well educated and know nothing about politics. Here in the country, the most interesting thing is a horse galloping through the village, or something like that. All I've ever done is drive trucks. Frozen meat, trees, that sort of thing. For the last few years, I've been delivering the mail. Why would I go to Dublin? It would be over my head; I would make a fool of myself."

When I visit Finbarr O'Brien years later, he shakes my hand and looks uncertain. He had assumed an interview request from a foreign country could only be some kind of prank call, he tells me. He was puzzled why someone from abroad would be interested in him. There are many good answers to that question. One is that his story holds a clue to a question that's currently troubling people from Washington to Berlin: What can be done to restore the public's trust in politics? Another answer is that Finbarr O'Brien's story demonstrates the power of institutionalized contact. When Caroline approached him in the café, Finbarr was the Irish version of the middle-aged, angry White man. Had he been American, he might well have voted for Trump, or for the AfD had he been German. He was sickened by politicians: They'd promise the sun, the moon, and the stars during their election campaigns, only to forget all about it afterward. They'd kiss children's heads before the elections but wouldn't greet you later. The way he saw it, they were too full of themselves, with their degrees and titles.

Caroline gave him her phone number in case he changed his mind. That evening, Finbarr received a dressing down from his eldest son. "Dad," he said, "this is a once-in-a-lifetime opportunity. You can't be ranting about the politicians and then, once you get a chance to do something about it, refuse." So he picked up the phone. When Caroline answered, Finbarr was hoping that she'd found someone else. She hadn't.

A few weeks later, on December 1, 2012, Finbarr stepped out of a taxi in the center of the Irish capital and looked up at the imposing façade of Dublin Castle. Once upon a time, kings resided here. In modern-day Ireland, the presidents take their oaths in these halls. That day, the Taoiseach—the prime minister of Ireland—was going to address the inaugural meeting of the Convention on the Constitution here. Finbarr was terrified.

Inside, everything was of enormous proportions: the rooms, the curtains, the chandeliers. The paintings told of events he knew nothing about. He entered an opulent hall arranged with rows and rows of chairs. He would have preferred to sit at the back, but his hearing wasn't great. Video footage of the day shows him sitting in the second row from the front, at the very end on the left. He's wearing a checked, short-sleeved shirt. Once, as the camera pans the audience, he's scratching his head.

Finbarr listened to the Taoiseach's opening speech, then to a man with a white beard—an economist—who had been appointed chairman of the assembly and who introduced himself as Tom Arnold. Sixty-six citizens, thirty-three politicians, and Tom Arnold. It was one hundred people in total. Onstage, Arnold said that the Irish had lost confidence in their elites. *That's true*, Finbarr remembers thinking. Arnold said that they had come together here to preserve democracy. He quoted the Irish Nobel laureate in Literature Seamus Heaney and added: "The shapers of the 1937 Constitution did a good job. Now it is our time and our turn." Finbarr had goosebumps.

The Taoiseach applauded, and so did his deputy, the Tánaiste; the members of parliament and the ministers; the whole room, including Finbarr. *What in God's name am I doing here?* he wondered.

A month later, on a Saturday morning in late January 2013, Finbarr found himself in a hotel north of Dublin, looking at an information board. He found his place, at table four. The subject of this first workshop was going to be electoral reform. Every month, they would discuss a different topic. In April, they were scheduled to discuss same-sex marriage.

Finbarr entered a huge conference room, decorated in Gaelic green. There were cameras at the back, a stage at the front, and large round tables that dotted the room. A few people were seated here and there, but table four, near the front, was still empty. Finbarr sat down.

A few moments later, a young man came up to the table. Two piercings glinted in his lips, the sides of his head were shaved, and a strip of spiky hair was left in the middle. Finbarr noticed the man's makeup and painted fingernails, every nail a different color of the rainbow. Finbarr thought, *The man is gay*. Up until this moment he had felt mainly nervous. Now, a familiar, overwhelming feeling took hold of his chest. He began to panic.

"What I thought was, 'I'll put that guy through the window.' My mind went wild. In my head I was back in my bedroom, I was nine, ten years old. As clearly as the pierced face of the man in front of me, I saw another man in front of my mind's eye, one with a perfectly knotted tie. I could smell the man's smoker's breath. It was many, many years ago and yet it felt like yesterday. He was a friend of my parents', and when he came to visit, they always invited him to stay the night. Every time, I hoped he'd say no, but he rarely said no. He would come to me, for about two years, again and again. I hoped that our house would come crushing down on our heads and bury us all."

Young Finbarr suffered the abuse in silence. He told no one, but his child's mind was racing. In those days, two very different things became indistinguishable to him from each other:

men who are sexually attracted to people of their own sex, and violence against children. Finbarr concluded that homosexuals are pedophiles. He wouldn't learn the words to express that thought until much later, but in those childhood days, the thought burned into his mind, quietly and unchallenged. Finbarr didn't even tell his parents what the man was doing to him. What he would have gotten from them, he imagines, was disbelief and a slap across the face. The man was like a god in their house.

It was all too much for him, far too much. As a teenager, he started to drink. He avoided people and went berserk if a man happened to touch him, even by accident. Like some veterans who are catapulted back to the battlefield by the slam of a car door, Finbarr would lash out at the mere sensation of a man's skin on his.

When he was old enough, he would sometimes drive to Cork, an hour away, where the man supposedly lived. He would spend hours prowling the streets, looking for him. If he had found him, he says now, he would have beaten him to death. Finbarr became a truck driver. Behind the wheel he could be alone with his thoughts. Once, when he was eighteen or so, he put a noose around his neck and jumped. "I shouldn't be here today," he tells me. But the rope broke. It injured his larynx. Ever since, his voice has been as rough as a drunkard's after an all-night binge.

Finbarr learned later that his abuser had killed himself. He decided he would tear down the headstone, but standing in front of it, he could only shake his head. Although this happened many years ago, the man continued to live in Finbarr's head, always there, always threatening. "Imagine you've got a scar that itches and itches, and all you want to do is scratch it. I have had this feeling for fifty years, in a place I can't reach, inside my head."

Finbarr got married, but he never told his wife what had happened. His sons grew into men, but he never told them either. For decades, no one had the opportunity to correct what he believed to be true since childhood: that there was only one place for gay men, and that was six feet under.

He was nearly fifty when this toxic thought was challenged for the first time. A therapist his doctor had recommended explained to him the difference between homosexuality and pedophilia. A simple distinction, really, but to him it was a revelation. The therapist taught him something else too. When he feels the panic rising, she said, he should lean back and take a good look around, then explain what he sees: the color of the walls, the themes of the paintings, the people in the room, what they look like, what they're wearing. That way, she said, he could bring himself back from the past and into the present, from a place of pain to a place of safety.

He used this trick all the time now. It felt like he had finally found a way to scratch that itch and soothe the pain, at least for a little while.

So when Finbarr learned that they would discuss same-sex marriage at the convention, he thought he was ready for it. He was even curious. He had never knowingly met a gay person, not since the abuse, and maybe the man hadn't even been gay, just a pedophile. Now that he knew the difference, he wasn't so sure anymore.

Finbarr was feeling a little lost in that huge hotel, grappling with the rules of the electoral system that was to be discussed during this first workshop weekend after the opening ceremony. But suddenly, catching sight of this man, piercings, fingernails, and all—he couldn't care less about any of it. *Lean back, look around*, he thought.

He noted the large hall, wood paneling on the walls, a brown-and-beige patterned carpet, people flocking into the room. The man with the pierced lips sat down opposite him, and it was all Finbarr could do to ignore him.

Chris Lyons was twenty-six when a friend's mother, who worked at a polling institute, emailed him and asked if he wanted to take part. By then, his sadness about not having equal rights as a gay man had turned into activism. He wanted to give Ireland another chance, he said at the time. "'Seriously, this is the first guy I'm meeting here?' I saw him staring at my fingernails; he was obviously uncomfortable. I had probably overdone the queer look: mohawk, eyeliner, fingernails; a little less would have done the trick as well. I looked at him. He stared into the air. 'Okay,' I thought, 'gentleman's agreement, you don't look at me, I don't look at you. No need for introductions. Your name tag says Finbarr O'Brien, mine says Chris Lyons.' In my head, this film started playing. Older Irish man, my whole life I've been fighting people like this and their values. Again and again, I've had to say, you know, I'm not a pervert, I am a fully valid human being. Even my mother thought I was a pedophile when I told her I was gay when I was seventeen. After I'd come out, my father drove me back to the university in Cork and told me never to come home again. In Cork, there was a pub where gays could party. The boys would be waiting outside. They would fill trash bags with beer glasses and throw them at us. Once, one of them caught me just so and cut open the back of my head. We laughed it off: 'Ha-ha, I've been glassed.' It was just so sad. Cork has the highest suicide rate among young people in the whole country."

Chris figured that if he didn't get full equal rights within the next two years, he would leave the country. He wanted the right to marry and to be allowed to adopt children, and if anything happened to him, God forbid, he wanted his children to inherit his property. He had already searched for houses in Canada.

"I didn't go to Dublin to beg for the right to marry. I went there to scream, 'Get the hell out of my way!' The convention would decide whether I was going to stay in Ireland or not. I wanted everyone to know that, and therefore, everyone needed to know that I was gay. So I dressed as the stereotypical gay man, even though I'd never normally do that. When I got there, all my confidence drained away. There were hardly any young people, lots of old Ireland. Walking through the room, I got scared. Then I found my table, and there was Finbarr."

In a way, both Finbarr O'Brien and Chris Lyons were the worst possible first person for the other to meet at the assembly. In an instant, they both triggered the other's traumatic experiences in a situation where they were both feeling vulnerable already. For a while they sat in silence until more people joined their table.

"A woman sat down next to me. I asked her who she was, and she said, 'What, you don't know who I am?' She was a politician, apparently. Then we went around the table introducing ourselves. I can't remember what Finbarr said, but I got the overall impression that everyone was much more grown-up than me, with careers and homes and cars. I was like a lost puppy.

When it was my turn, I didn't know what to say, so I just said what was on my mind: that I felt out of place, that I was scared. Opposite me, Finbarr started nodding vigorously."

"Chris said exactly what I was thinking!" said Finbarr. "The others gave the impression that they did this sort of thing every day. Chris and I were different. It was weird; he was just like I had pictured a homosexual, but he was so honest and authentic."

Chris said, "I could see the effect my words were having on Finbarr, so I continued. I said I didn't know why I was there, among all these important people. Finbarr nearly climbed across the table to me in agreement. Then he said, 'I feel exactly like Chris.' That was one of the most clarifying moments of my life, and I decided I'd spend the weekends here with Finbarr. I don't care if he's a homophobe; I'll deal with that later."

In a way, Finbarr O'Brien and Chris Lyons were both also the best possible first person for the other to meet, except that neither of them realized it yet. During their first break they made small talk. At lunch they sat together. At dinner they laughed about something that had happened earlier in the day, when experts were giving speeches about voting rights, with complicated formulas and graphs. At some point, the speaker had asked the audience if everyone had understood. One hand went up: Finbarr O'Brien's, and he said, no, he now understood less than before. The speaker replied, no problem, they would proceed only as fast as the slowest horse in the stable, which Finbarr had laughed off congenially. And then they had explained it again, and Chris was glad because, in truth, he hadn't taken it all in either.

In the evening they had some beers at the bar. Finbarr's fear had not disappeared entirely, but he sensed how his therapist's words began to resonate with reality. He continued to be amazed by the discrepancy between Chris's appearance, which was exactly as he had expected, and his manner, which was so different from how he'd imagined homosexuals to be, so normal.

At the convention weekends, Finbarr and Chris would talk late into the night, about Finbarr's grandchildren, about Chris's job in IT, about the topics to be discussed on Ireland's constitution. Should the length of the president's term of office be cut back from seven years to five? Should the voting age be reduced from eighteen to seventeen? At first, they often discussed the politicians at the convention and the fact that there were tables at lunch where they kept to themselves.

Essentially, they were all politicians here. As chairman, Tom Arnold had a special role, but the other ninety-nine were equals, senators and mailmen alike. Except, according to Finbarr and Chris, the thirty-three behaved differently from the sixty-six. It wouldn't have occurred to Finbarr to do what one politician did, when she grabbed the microphone and talked for ages without saying anything. It was bizarre; they were all listening to her, and after she sat down everyone continued as if nothing had happened. Her aim, apparently, wasn't to drive the debate forward; she just wanted visibility.

Finbarr couldn't have cared less about visibility. He asked questions when he didn't understand and gave answers when he was asked a question. He wanted to do justice to the individual topics and was glad when he could do so in silence.

But as the convention went on, the distinction between the thirty-three and the sixty-six became more blurred. At mealtimes, the groups started to intermingle. Sometimes Chris and one of the politicians would travel back home together on the train and chat.

Over time, the conversations between Finbarr and Chris also changed and turned to more personal issues. Chris told Finbarr about his coming out and that his mother thought he was a pedophile, while his father's only concern was to keep it secret, when all Chris wanted to do was shout it out to the world with pride.

Finbarr realized that he had fallen for another fallacy, one that even his therapist had not been able to dispel. When he thought about homosexuality, he instantly conjured up images of men doing things to each other that revolted him. To him, homosexuality was sexuality. Now, however, he understood that it was not primarily about sex, but about love, family, and everyday life. Chris sensed that Finbarr also needed to get something off his chest.

"He always went back to when we first met: 'Chris, remember on the first day? I didn't know where to look . . .' Eventually, I realized that he kept returning to that situation because there was something else he wanted to say. He did tell me in the end. The conversation started as it always did, but then he kept on going. He didn't tell me everything, but enough for me to understand."

For the other attendees at the convention, the friendship between the young gay man, whose haircut took on a different shape and color each month, and the old mailman became something to talk about. After several months, Chris was no longer as defeatist about the same-sex marriage vote. He was pretty sure that he had won Finbarr over, so he was hopeful that it had worked for others too.

Same-sex marriage was on the agenda in April 2013. The debates were to be held on a Saturday, followed by the vote on Sunday. That weekend, Finbarr sat at a table near the front, Chris a few tables away. On the stage, experts and lobbyists spoke about the well-being of children and the right to adopt, and about biology and theology. At the back of the room, journalists tapped away on their laptops.

In a way, the assembly was exactly like a parliament, a representation of the people, except that its members hadn't been elected, but chosen at random. And yet the difference could not have been greater. No one was playing on their phone or chatting with their neighbor. A few people were taking notes. There were no howls of protest, no rhetoric, no drama, and no ritualized exchange of predefined viewpoints. The citizens didn't belong to any parties that told them which opinions to uphold. Everyone wrestled with their own conscience, alone. Among them were some who changed their minds three times a day after hearing three different arguments for and against. More contributions to the debate ended with a question mark than with an exclamation point.

Later, when I was sitting in the Dublin conference room among my Irish colleagues and watching the citizens at work, I felt very humble. These weren't your custom-made suit–wearing, briefcase-toting types; this was the real Ireland. Here were suits that were too big or too small and hadn't been worn for a while. Here were T-shirts and sneakers, chunky glasses, and teased hair. The room was humming with the music of thick regional accents. At the tables, teachers and social workers, masons and ministers, employed and unemployed were all coming together. It was democratic chaos, in a good way; nothing was taken for granted. I imagined that these strangers might become friends and marveled at how the most important office in a democracy, that of the citizen, was filled with new meaning.

In recent years, in addition to the Irish, many other European citizens have felt that they are not represented by their parliaments. It begins with the fact that the members of, say, the Bundestag in Germany, the House of Commons in the UK, or the *Assemblée nationale* in France do not look like the people they represent. Among their numbers are far more lawyers than in the general population, more university graduates, fewer blue-collar workers, fewer ethnic minorities, hardly any tradespeople, typically more men than women, and more people over sixty than under thirty. Also, lawmakers are usually career politicians. Often they move from one job to the next, secretary of this, senator for that, then a few years in the opposition before they're back in government. Many politicians do this for decades. They all know each other and meet up regularly. One might argue that representatives, who are supposed to *represent* the diversity in society, have become a homogeneous group with a common phenotype. They wear the same suits and blazers, they have the same gestures, and they casually utter the same soundbites in front of the cameras.

Such homogeneity is a shaky foundation for effective representation. How much further is that foundation undermined when the differences between the representatives and the represented go beyond gestures and appearances and become charged with content; when most representatives hold one opinion and the majority of the people another?

• • •

When Angela Merkel, then the chancellor of Germany, decided in the summer of 2015 to leave the borders open to refugees, her decision was welcomed by all the parties represented in the Bundestag. Yet, in a survey run by a German polling institute, 41 percent of respondents agreed with the statement that Germany could not cope with such large numbers of refugees.[1] Projected onto the electorate, this translates to twenty-five million citizens of voting age. Those twenty-five million people were not represented by their parliament when it came to arguably the most important political issue at the time.

No matter how right Merkel's decision may have been from an ethical, moral, or humanitarian viewpoint, it is dangerous for a representative democracy if millions of people don't have anyone who speaks for them. If they had representatives who voiced their concerns as part of the democratic process, they would have had no reason to doubt democracy. But that's not what happened. Millions of people felt politically abandoned. As a result, they went over to far-right groups and parties like the AfD whose political leaders may appear downright scary but who gave millions the feeling that they were being heard.

In a democracy, it isn't good enough for the government to do the right thing. A government must also convince those it governs that it is doing the right thing. Today, Germany remains divided, with a large part of the public feeling politically unrepresented, as is the case in many Western nations.

One man believes he has found a solution to this institutional crisis. Born in 1971, David Van Reybrouck is a historian and archaeologist who speaks eight languages. He is Belgian, and that is one of the reasons the concept of democracy is so important to him. Not that long ago, Belgium spent 540 days without a government. The rest of Europe laughed about this strange country, but to Van Reybrouck the Belgian crisis was more than just a curiosity. He read Aristotle, Plato, Montesquieu, and Madison, and realized that one of the philosophers' central concepts of democracy had somehow been forgotten over the last few centuries.

In fact, most stable democracies in history, such as the city-state of Athens in ancient Greece, were quite different from the ones that are in crisis today. It's not just that the ancient Greeks didn't have social media or that their women were excluded from politics. The crucial difference is that the members of the Athens government, the so-called boule, were not elected; they were chosen by lottery.

It sounds bizarre today, but at the time, it was the only sensible solution. Terms of office were limited, and most Athenians held a political office at some point in their lives, which eradicated the distinction between citizens and politicians, the governing and the governed, those at the top and those at the bottom. The people governed themselves. There were no issues of representation, no election campaigns, and no broken promises. The lottery made everyone equal.

To the Athenians, a caste of besuited career politicians would have seemed absurd. Politics at the time was all about addressing the matters of the day, not about personal advancement or self-assertion. Only a handful of positions were elected, in the military and in finance, for example. On all other issues, the people should have the say, ordinary people, regardless of their education or occupation, and a random draw was considered the most reliable system to appoint them.

In the fourth century BCE, Aristotle wrote, "It is thought to be democratic for the offices to be assigned by lot, for them to be elected oligarchic."[2] For centuries, these words endured as a principle of political philosophy. Democracy meant appointment by lottery. It was no different in the Italian city-states of Venice and Florence during the Renaissance. In the middle of the eighteenth century, Montesquieu reiterated Aristotle's idea: "The suffrage by lot is natural to democracy; as that by choice is to aristocracy."[3] A few years later, in 1762, Jean-Jacques Rousseau wrote in his influential book *The Social Contract*: "In any real democracy, magistracy isn't a benefit—it's a burdensome responsibility that can't fairly be imposed on one individual rather than another. If the individual is selected by a lottery, the selection is being made by the law that establishes the lottery."[4]

Then something astonishing happened. In America and France, the people were tearing down the supremacies of crown and absolutism; the revolutionaries demanded democracy. Their leaders, however, were skeptical. Could the people really govern themselves, they wondered? Would it not be better to concentrate power in the hands of a few—ideally their own?

In 1776 John Adams, a wealthy lawyer, wrote: "The first step to be taken then, is to depute power from the many to a few of the most wise and virtuous."[5]

Thomas Jefferson, a lawyer and the son of a prosperous plantation owner, wrote: "There is a natural aristocracy among men. The grounds of this are virtue and talents. . . . May we not even say that that form of government is the best which provides the most effectually for a pure selection of these natural aristoi into the offices of government?"[6]

And the philosopher James Madison, the son of a rich tobacco farmer, pronounced: "Who are to be the objects of popular choice? Every citizen whose merit may recommend him to the esteem and confidence of his country. No qualification of wealth, of birth, of religious faith, or of civil profession, is permitted to fetter the judgment or disappoint the inclination of the people."[7]

Adams, Jefferson, and Madison had identified the perfect system for a popular sovereignty where power is shared by only a very small section of the people: elections. Who else would the American people choose if not the wisest, the brightest, and the wealthiest? John Adams went on to become the first vice president of the United States under George Washington, and in 1779 was elected president himself. Thomas Jefferson followed in 1801 and James Madison in 1809.

The sixth US president's name was Adams again, John Adams's son John Quincy. The Adamses became the first American political dynasty, followed over a century later by the Kennedys, the Bushes, and the Clintons.

Across the Atlantic, in France, the revolution was likewise hijacked by the bourgeoisie. The priest and novelist Emmanuel-Joseph Sieyès, whose pamphlet *What Is the Third Estate?* had helped galvanize the people for the storming of the Bastille, wrote less than two months after the event: "In a country that is not a democracy—and France cannot be one—the people, I repeat, can speak or act only through its representatives."[8]

Looking at these events through the lens of history, we realize that what we call a revolution today was, in fact, merely the replacement of one type of aristocracy (inherited) with another (electoral). The old elite lost their power to the new elite, and the people were sold this new system as democracy. In what was one of the greatest public relations coups in history, a concept that for more than two thousand years had been characterized by a lottery system had been redefined.

These electoral aristocracies turned out to be extraordinarily stable, partly because over time they became increasingly democratic. The right to vote was extended to more groups until almost everyone was allowed to take part. Workers' parties began to emerge, fighting for ordinary people to be allowed to rise to the top of the political ranks. Some countries introduced tools such as propositions and referendums to consult their citizens. Generally, however, a class of career politicians ruled the land.

This model became so entrenched over the centuries that when a simple mailman like Finbarr O'Brien was asked if he'd like to participate in politics, his automatic response was, "I'm not educated enough." To him there was no question that politics was reserved for the intelligent ones, for the elites.

In his book *Against Elections*,[9] David Van Reybrouck offers a solution for the problems of our democracy. As the title suggests, he proposes a return to the origins of democracy, to the lottery system, to allow some room for chance in the political process. That's what they did in Ireland, where in the space of a few weeks the citizens' assembly had not only managed to instill a fresh enthusiasm for politics in a disenchanted older White man but was also well on its way to changing the country as a whole.

• • •

Sitting in the hotel conference room, Finbarr O'Brien felt well informed as the debate over same-sex marriage began that Saturday morning in April 2013. After many conversations with Chris, he was aware of most of the arguments. He had changed his mind, not only about Chris but about gay men in general. Chris had achieved with Finbarr what the Roma family had failed to do with Harald and Christa Hermes. What had he done differently?

Social psychologists have established that two conditions ought to be met for the behavior of one person to rub off on an entire group and for that person to be regarded not as the exception but the rule. Unknowingly, Chris had met both of those conditions. On the day he and Finbarr first met, Chris had transformed himself into a near-comical, inflated, gay cliché. Something he initially regretted, thinking he might have gone too far, had actually worked in his favor.

When Finbarr first caught sight of Chris, his mind instantly read his optical impulses as: *This is not just a man, but a gay man.* Chris was so loaded with cliché that it never occurred to Finbarr to regard him as an exception. The more representative an individual appears for a group, the harder it is to discount them as a one-off.

Chris also fulfilled the second condition. He was the very first gay man Finbarr had knowingly met, not the second or third or tenth. Had Finbarr met others first and gotten a different impression of them, or had those others confirmed Finbarr's negative prejudices, Chris would have had to compete with them, and it would have been much more difficult for him to sway Finbarr's prejudices. But that wasn't the case; he was the first, and the road was clear for him.

Finbarr was pretty sure that he would vote for the legalization of same-sex marriage the following day, not just for Chris's sake but for all gay men. There was just one thing that bothered him: the question of children. How could two men have children together? And would they not get bullied at school? Was it fair to the children? Then a young woman took to the stage, and Finbarr's senses sharpened.

> Good afternoon, everyone. My name is Claire O'Connell, and I'm twenty-two years old. I study medicine . . . and I live in Dublin with my younger sister Dee and our two parents. . . . We're a typical Irish household, [except] my parents are two women. And people often ask what it's like being raised by two mommies. I fear my answer often disappoints them because the truth is that my childhood was fairly ordinary. It wasn't very different from that of my friends because, growing up, I had what every child needs: loving parents. They were there to bandage my knees when I fell and to wipe my tears when I cried. And people often asked: Was I bullied in school because I had two moms? Again, I disappoint them because I have had the typical school experience. I was never afraid to tell anyone my mom was gay. I was never bullied because of it. Was I ever worried what my friends would think? Actually, most people just thought it was cool that I had two moms. In fact, the running joke among my friends is that my family was the most normal out of anyone's we know.

Finbarr decided he would vote "yes." Then representatives of the church started to speak. Nature had made man and woman, they argued. It was the only way to bring children into the world, they said. A Catholic bishop talked about how deeply the church cared for the institution of marriage, how immensely precious it was, and that it was now at stake. Finbarr thought of the many boys who had been abused by priests just as he had been abused as a child, and how the church had looked the other way and simply shifted offenders to different positions, where they would go on to abuse more boys.[10] And yet, this bishop had the nerve to act as a moral authority, Finbarr thought angrily. He was shaking with rage. He had to speak up now; he had to say something to counter the bishop's argument. He would never forgive himself if he didn't.

And suddenly there he was, Finbarr O'Brien, in a ruby-red sweater over a white shirt, his right hand clutching the microphone. A camera zoomed in on him, his words being livestreamed over the internet. He had not prepared what he would say, Finbarr remembers; the words just came to him. "The biggest problem is ignorance. People don't know enough. I was just the same. Many years ago, I suffered abuse, and after that the two things were the same to me: gay men and abuse. I just didn't know any better. But now I've learned that homosexuals, men and women, are normal people."

He didn't say which way he was going to vote the next day, but everyone in the room knew. After the meeting he headed straight for the bar and downed a double whiskey. Then people started coming up to him to congratulate him; one after the other they wanted to shake his hand.

On Sunday, seventy-nine members of the assembly voted for the amendment to the constitution. Seventy-nine percent voted for the legalization of same-sex marriage in one of the most Catholic and most conservative countries in Europe.

It is difficult to say exactly how much of this was because of Finbarr O'Brien. Chris Lyons says that it was more than just the one ballot paper that his friend put in the box. Finbarr's speech inspired others to follow him, he says. People who were in the room that day say that his speech had a cathartic effect on them. They had hung on Finbarr's every word because they could see that he was being utterly authentic, there were no pretenses, no omissions, no lies, and they loved that about him. In this respect, Chris says, Finbarr was the exact opposite of a politician.

But did that very fact not make him an outstanding politician? Was Finbarr's reaction not the essence of politics, striking a chord with voters by using the right words and one's own personality, being so authentic that others are inspired to follow you?

When I interviewed some of those who were there at the time—a teacher from Dublin, a dancer from Kildare, a social worker from Wexford, a political scientist from University College Dublin, and the chairman, Tom Arnold—there always came a point where they urged me to talk to a mailman from Macroom by the name of Finbarr. Finbarr O'Brien, the man who preferred to remain invisible, may have been the most visible person at the convention.

The Irish parliament respected the convention's vote on same-sex marriage and called a referendum—the only means for amending the constitution. Following the citizens' recommendation, all big parties spoke out in favor of legalization. On May 22, 2015, two years after the convention's ballot, Ireland went to the polls. Without realizing it, that day the Irish electorate was also deciding whether their fellow citizen Chris Lyons would remain in the country or leave.

Chris Lyons often found himself moved to tears in those days, he remembers. When scrolling through his Twitter feed, he saw endless images with the hashtag #hometovote: Irish men and women, young and old, from all over the world were returning to Ireland to vote. They were coming from Australia, the United States, the United Kingdom. Photos showed them sitting on planes and getting off buses, many carrying rainbow flags in their hands. In a way Chris felt as if these people were coming home for him, as if they wanted to atone for all his suffering and make him a valid member of society at last.

Finbarr watched the referendum coverage on TV. In the morning, he and his wife had gone to the polling station, where he had voted for the legalization of same-sex marriage a second time. He didn't know where his wife had marked her "X"; he assumed "No," the same as he expected for most people in the village. Judging by what the people had been saying at the pub, he didn't think Chris would stay in Ireland after all. Eventually, the news anchor announced the result: 62 percent in favor. On TV, people in the streets of Dublin, dressed in all the colors of the rainbow, were crying tears of joy.

Today, Finbarr talks about politics as an insider. Sometimes, in the pub he even finds himself defending politicians. In the United States, in Germany, and in many other countries, people are asking how the public's trust in politics can be restored. With Finbarr O'Brien it started with politics having trust in him.

Could the result of the Irish experiment be any more encouraging? Finbarr O'Brien and Chris Lyons, a homophobe and a homosexual, have become friends. A former enraged citizen now comes to the defense of politicians in the pub. Sixty-six citizens and thirty-three politicians largely put aside their prejudices. Many of them now rave about the experience, consequentially injecting more democratic spirit into society. None of that would have happened if it hadn't been for the democratic lottery, if the Irish government hadn't decided to call a convention on the constitution and, in the process, brought a diverse group of strangers into contact with each other.

Looking back, Finbarr says, there's only one thing that bothers him: that he wasn't allowed to take part in the second convention, the Citizens' Assembly established in 2016, this time without any politicians. Ninety-nine citizens and a chairwoman got together to discuss several political issues. Their most important topic, abortion, was even more controversial than same-sex marriage, and was the subject of discussion for a full five months. At the end, the assembly voted in favor of overturning the ban imposed by the constitution. The government called a referendum, and in May 2018 the Irish people overwhelmingly endorsed the assembly's proposal.

• • •

In a diverse society, there is likely no more reliable tool for bringing people with opposing views together than a random draw. In Ireland, the plan was used on a relatively small scale: only a hundred people, only advisory, and still it had huge repercussions. In theory, lotteries could be used on a much grander, more radical scale. Entire representative bodies could be appointed by lotteries: the German Bundestag, the British House of Commons, and the US Congress. In 2019, the German-speaking region of East Belgium introduced a permanent political council whose members are drafted by lottery; in 2022, the German city of Aachen is following suit. A lottery system can also be applied in other, nonpolitical areas of life.

At universities across the United States, for example, students commonly live on campus, sharing a room with another student. Some universities no longer permit freshmen to choose their roommate but instead allocate random pairs together. This creates "more colorful" room shares, where before there tended to be ethnic homogeneity in the dorms.

In his 1954 book *The Nature of Prejudice*, Gordon W. Allport relates an anecdote about the dean of a girls' college, who on the first day of a new term received two furious visitors: "They were students from the South who found that in the small dormitory to which they were assigned a [Black] student was also assigned. They demanded that she be moved out. The dean thought for a moment and then said, 'Well, we have a rule that girls may not change their dormitory assignments when they are once made for the year; but in this case I'll make an exception. You girls may move out if you wish and go to another house.' The girls were taken aback. But they did not move, for their training told them that a [Black person] should get out of their way. Staying on, a bit grimly at first, they soon found that their feelings of hostility against their [Black] housemate lessened; by the end of the term they were good friends with her."[11]

The episode reads as if the dean was a friend of the author, who told the story to Allport, who consequently, considering it relevant, included it in his book, even though it had no scientific validity. Today, over seventy years later, we know that it does indeed have scientific validity. The social psychologists Sarah

E. Gaither and Samuel R. Sommers concluded in a study that White students sharing a room with a non-White student had, after four months, a more diverse circle of friends and generally attached a higher value to diversity than those living with a White roommate. After six months, their behavior indicated that they were less anxious and more pleasant when interacting with non-White individuals.[12]

The Harvard economist Gautam Rao studied the effect of a policy change in India. In Delhi, exclusive private schools for upper-class children had been mandated to accept children from poor families. Rao found that wealthy children mixing with poor classmates became less likely to discriminate against poor students and more generous toward them. They were also more likely to engage in charitable activities.[13]

One might argue that contact on campus or in high school is too late. The two Southern girls in Allport's anecdote and the rich children in Delhi show that over the first ten to twenty years of their lives, students have already developed deeply rooted prejudices that can only be eliminated with a certain effort. Should we not start sooner, before these prejudices become entrenched or even take hold?

Some large American cities have started an interesting experiment. Based on the model by the Nobel laureate in Economics Alvin Roth, cities like San Francisco and Washington, DC, have developed a system to allocate students to elementary schools at random. Inner-city elementary schools are highly segregated by ethnicity and social background. In some neighborhoods, there are schools near each other whose student bodies could not be more different. One may have only White, middle-class children, while the other has only Black children from a low-income background. Or one may have mostly children who speak only English at home, while the other has only children who speak English as a second language.

Starting with elementary school students has many advantages. Children don't follow any ideologies. They make friends quickly. And as a best-case scenario, their experiences will lead them to become empathy ambassadors who will magnify the effect when they enter society as adults. It may even be a way for society to be vaccinated against hatred.

6

The Neighbors

How our choice of home determines our lives

Silvia Knaus had always found Warth too parochial. With a population of six hundred in northeastern Switzerland, the only public transportation is a twice-hourly bus that delivers the mail and also takes passengers. Her mother used to busy herself in the kitchen, and her father worked at the pig farm at the local monastery. On rare days off, the Knaus family went on hikes, starting and ending at their front door. As a kid, Silvia sometimes asked her mother where various objects came from: the TV, the hamburger, the car. Her mother's answer was always the same, "From America." Everything came from America. Nothing came from here, the Swiss region of Thurgau, Silvia remembers thinking. Certainly nothing came from Warth.

At eighteen-and-a-half, Silvia got on a plane, leaving Switzerland for the first time. Her destination: America. She'll be back soon, the people in her village said. And she was, albeit briefly. Then it was back to America, and on to Australia. She then moved to Zurich, not that far geographically, but in every other aspect a million miles away: a city teeming with people, parties, movie theaters, trains, trolleys, and buses—and not just twice hourly.

The elevator stopped between split-level floors, and to get to the apartment she shared with a friend, Silvia had to climb half a dozen steps. It wasn't a problem, until one day it was. Her legs simply stopped working. In her mid-twenties, Silvia was where she wanted to be, in the city and in life, but she could no longer climb those steps.

As a child at school, she had always had the messiest handwriting of everyone in her class. Some children are just clumsy, she used to say. Every year she'd gone to ski camp, but while the others gradually improved and eventually became great skiers, she kept wobbling on her skis like a beginner. I'm just not very good at sports, she'd said.

Now she was given a diagnosis: Friedreich's ataxia. The FXN gene, on chromosome nine, was responsible for interrupted communication between the spinal cord and the cerebellum, loss of sensation in the arms and legs, and degeneration of the muscles. It was not a death sentence, she remembers the neurologist saying, but it wasn't going to get any better either.

It's hard to comprehend how much we rely on our muscles, not just for climbing stairs but also for forming words. Silvia's speech became flat; some syllables lost their vowels. One day, she was talking on the phone with a client at the call center where she worked: "Please press the pound key," she tried to say.

"Pardon?"

"Please press the [indistinguishable]."

"Pardon?" She realized that she had reached her limit and resigned.

At twenty-nine, she needed a wheelchair and went back to Warth. For the next year she traveled, pulling out all the stops: South Africa, St. Helena, a road trip to Norway, Hong Kong, Macau, Australia, and back to Warth again—twenty countries in one year, a last hurrah. Who knows how much longer she'd be able to. Her childhood friends now had children of their own and withdrew into their homes in the evenings, while Silvia sat in her old bedroom at home, alone. She would often go to Zurich in the morning and return in the evening, but she didn't make any friends. "It's difficult in a wheelchair," she said.

The few wheelchair-accessible apartments in Zurich, advertised online, cost upward of three thousand Swiss francs (more than $3,000) per month. Her disability pension would cover rent up to seventeen hundred francs. At the train station one evening, she picked up a copy of *Blick*, a trashy but free tabloid. Reading on the train, she learned that a housing cooperative was developing a residential complex right in the middle of the city, with small but affordable apartments and large communal areas. The architecture of Kalkbreite, as the building was to be called, was designed to facilitate contact between the residents, Silvia read. Inexpensive accommodation in the city and social interaction—if she had understood the article correctly, this place would combine two of her deepest aspirations.

"We already have more applicants than spaces," the voice on the phone said. Silvia applied anyway. The article had said that diversity mattered to the co-op. Maybe her wheelchair would prove to be a bonus for once. It did.

In July 2014, Silvia moved in. She brought a bed, a wardrobe, and a small table. At just over 300 square feet, there was little space for anything else. But the apartment came with the rare convenience of a wheelchair-accessible kitchen, including a stovetop and a fridge. If she wanted to use an oven, she could use the communal one in the lounge next door, which she shared with eleven other residents. Together, they were Cluster Two. None of the twelve apartments had an oven or a washing machine. Near the entrance, there was a shared laundry room for everyone's use. *So what*, Silvia thought, at least she was back in the city.

I first visit Kalkbreite in the fall of 2018. Beforehand, I had read that the house naturally brings people into contact. Judging from my own experience, I considered this to be marketing nonsense. The city apartment blocks where I had lived had all been of different designs and yet had all resulted in the same urban anonymity. I barely knew some of my neighbors by sight, let alone by name.

Getting off at the streetcar stop at Kalkbreite, I find myself in front of a building that resembles a cream-colored ocean liner. In what would be the hull of the ship, three stories tall, there is a movie theater called Houdini, an organic supermarket, and a few shops. Between a fancy Turkish restaurant, where people are reading the newspapers, and a cozy-looking bar, a monumental staircase leads to a raised inner courtyard, where children are playing on swings. Around the courtyard, four floors of apartments rise up like the decks of a ship, the homes of the building's two hundred and fifty residents.

Walking into the main entrance area feels like entering a hotel lobby—which it is, in a way. The receptionist who greets me also manages the twelve bedrooms that serve as guest rooms for the residents. Since there is little space in the small apartments for overnight guests, visitors can stay in the guest rooms on the ground floor. There's no need to make up a daybed or wash the sheets—something the residents tell me they appreciate.

The lobby is the lifeline of the building. It leads to the cafeteria, where I see people sitting and chatting. Off to the side are the residents' mailboxes, where a young man in a hat is talking with an elderly woman. At the back there is a seating area with sofas and floor-to-ceiling bookshelves. I later learn that the books are looked after by Erika, a trained librarian, now retired, who has a penchant for feminist literature and lives on the seventh floor. From the lobby, a flight of stairs leads to the second floor, where a wide corridor runs through the whole building. The residents call it *Rue Intérieure*, Inner Street. The name is apt; it's all happening here. Children are zooming around on scooters, and apartment doors are opening and closing. Silvia's room is here too. On the other floors, there is a yoga room, a music studio, a gym, a workshop, and on the top floor, next to the entrance to the roof terrace with its herb garden, there is a sauna. Most of these amenities are financed by the residents.

The architectural idea behind the residential hub is a kind of push and pull. The apartments are too small and furnished too sparsely for the residents to spend all their time in them, at least for those who bake, do the laundry, or entertain guests every now and then. At the same time, the communal areas are large, comfortable, and well equipped—in a word, welcoming.

The sign on the first door I stop at reads, "Frederike Bertschi, Cellist." The bell is waist-high, not a button to push but a small, golden handle that twists like an old corkscrew. Inside, I hear a mechanical noise that sounds like a bicycle bell, but not as shrill. Frederike is a woman in her sixties, slim, with a slight stoop. She invites me in, and we sit down at a small table by the window.

Frederike tells me that she comes from Winterthur, northeast of Zurich, from a conservative family. She studied classical music and played with orchestras in Flensburg and Nuremberg for many years. When she moved to Kalkbreite in 2014, all she knew of Zurich was the opera house, which she used to visit twice a week as a student, and the Zürichberg area with its million-dollar mansions dating back to the nineteenth century. One of her fellow students had lived there. This part of Zurich, the very left-wing Aussersihl district was new to her.

It took her a while to get used to the fact that at Kalkbreite, everyone—without exception—spoke to each other informally, using the German "du," she says. Sometimes in the hallways, she would come across people who would have frightened her in the past. Like this one guy who was overweight and had piercings everywhere, who drank too much, and was always lugging around a heavy bag. It turns out, he was a friendly, sensitive man, she admits, but then he died at only fifty-eight. She often thinks about him, she says.

After twenty minutes or so, we are interrupted by the jingle of the doorbell, which on this side of the door consists of a little golden bell. Over the coming days, this jingling becomes the sound of the building to me. Every apartment has such a doorbell—except for one, as I will find out later. Outside Frederike's door, on Rue Intérieure, is a blonde woman in a wheelchair. She's wearing fashionable horn-rimmed glasses and a blue sweater. I hear the woman ask Frederike if she could help her put up some curtains later.

"You see," Frederike says as she returns, "that was my neighbor Silvia. At first, I avoided her. I had never met someone in a wheelchair before, and I didn't have the guts to talk to her. But now, when I'm at a public restroom I always register whether they are accessible for wheelchair users or not."

That's how I meet Silvia—I'm the one putting up her curtains two hours later. While I'm up on the ladder, she tells me about Warth and how Kalkbreite has helped her overcome her loneliness. I ask her how many people she knows here, *really* knows. She thinks for a moment and then rattles off a list: "Frederike, Claudia, Jamila, Madeleine, Fred, Sabur, Thomas, Regula, the other Regula, Doro, Stefan, Beat, Corinne, Françoise, Jonas . . . oh, I probably know two hundred people here. Except for the shared apartments—there's too much turnover; there are some I don't know." She's forever calling on her neighbors and asking for help, she says: Frederike, for example, or Tato, the young Brazilian masseur who lives across the hallway.

There's a pair of yellow-and-green flip-flops outside Tato's door. I ring the bell, but there's no answer. I get to meet him the following day as I walk down Rue Intérieure and peek into the sewing room. Inside, a young man with a hipster mustache is ironing a white shirt. It's decorated with two images of red masks that would suit a serial killer and a superhero alike. Tato tells me that the shirt was designed by his friend Pablo, a Spanish fashion designer who lives upstairs in the shared "True Love" apartment.

Tato talks about the "Kalkbreite spirit" and confirms that it's easy to get to know a lot of people here, and a very eclectic mix at that. Not knowing that I have already met Silvia and Frederike, he mentions that there is someone who uses a wheelchair in his cluster who sometimes helps him write letters. As a masseur, he says, he is always touching people, but he had to move here to learn what paralyzed legs feel like. There are also three retirees in his cluster, he adds and shrugs. "What did I know about life as a retiree?" Now, he says, he likes to sit in the sun with them, drinking wine together, and listening to them talk of the theater or of their shopping trips to Milan.

After a few days at Kalkbreite, I begin to change my mind. Maybe, in this case, naturally enforced contact is more than just marketing nonsense after all. Tato and Silvia, Tato and the retirees, Silvia and Frederike, Frederike and the man with the piercings. They have sewing classes and cards evenings, a film club and a group that looks after the sixty thousand honey-bees that live on the roof. At one point during the reporting, my recorder breaks, and within five minutes, Silvia has found me another. She knew that Jonas on the fifth floor records au-diobooks, and he had one. The people here really do know one another well—indeed, so well that some residents are fed up with it.

One young mother tells me that she is sending her daughter to a nursery a couple of streets away instead of to the in-house one. Otherwise, she says, she would never leave this microcosm, adding that it's just like living in a village, with all the pros and cons that that entails. Another resident quips that all that was missing was an undertaker, and all one's needs from the cradle to the grave would be met from within these walls. There is a birthing center, a nursery, a medical clinic, several health care professionals, and a small supermarket.

Then I learn that Kalkbreite not only tries to enforce contact between people, it's also trying to control who those people are. Item 2.1 of the leasing regulations states that the makeup of the residents with respect to "gender, age, income, professional and educational background, as well as nationality" should reflect that of the general population. Just as the convention in Dublin aimed to be a demographic mini-Ireland, Kalkbreite aspires to be a mini-Switzerland, except that the people here don't spend just one weekend a month together but every single day.

When you look around your own neighborhood, it becomes apparent just how revolutionary this idea is. In the area of Hamburg where I live, for example, I don't see many old people, even though there are more than twenty million retirees in Germany. I don't see many overweight people, either, even though nearly one in four adults in the country is obese. Instead, I see strollers and English-language signs advertising vegan cakes and Scandinavian-roast coffee.

It's the same in other countries too. When I interviewed Jamal, the reformed would-be terrorist in his Aarhus suburb, I saw dozens of döner kebab shops and people dressed in cheap clothes. When I interviewed John Gunther Dean, the Eleven Forty-Two veteran, in the sixteenth arrondissement in Paris, I saw people in designer clothes in fancy cafés eating croissants for fifteen dollars apiece. Recently, a London-based friend of mine told me how she had mentioned to someone that she bikes to work in the city. They were stunned—because they had immediately understood that living close enough to cycle to work in the City of London means that she must be among the top earners in British society. (She is.)

"Where do you live?" In large cities, the question can be a quick identity check. Sometimes you don't even need to see the person to get an immediate idea of what they are like: rich or poor, left-wing or right-wing, old or young. The names of neighborhoods become a code; geographical terms have become synonymous with social milieus, political attitudes, and living environments.

Sometimes these connotations change; urban sociologists talk about gentrification, for example, or its opposite, abandonment. Except during periods of transition, when the different groups mix because one hasn't fully left while the other hasn't fully moved in yet, it's often true that a neighborhood can be predominantly blue-collar workers, immigrants, hipsters, middle-class, students, etc. A research paper commissioned by the German Federal Ministry for Social Affairs concludes that the larger the city, the more profound the ethnic and social segregation.[1]

At a personal level, that's not a bad thing at all. I enjoy meeting new people in my favorite café and quickly establishing common areas of interest. But for society as a whole, it's a problem. There are few things that impact our daily lives more than where we live. It determines not only whom we meet in cafés, but also which nursery schools our children attend and what kind of parents and children we get to know there. It determines which sports clubs we join and who our teammates are. It determines who sits next to us in the waiting room at the doctor's and whom we talk to in the line at the post office. Where we live also often determines who our friends are. The more segregated the cities, the more homogeneous and bubble-like the living environments—and the more numerous the prejudices against the residents of other neighborhoods. The reverse is true as well: The more diverse the people living side by side in an area, the fewer prejudices the individuals are likely to have of the others. That's what makes Kalkbreite so interesting. It's located in Zürich's Kreis 4, a district known for its young, left-wing scene, with alternative clubs and art house theaters. Could Kalkbreite really be an island of demographic diversity amid these rather homogeneous surroundings? Is it possible to overturn the natural law of urban segmentation simply by writing diversification into the leasing regulations?

Having spent several days at Kalkbreite, I make a list of all the people I have met so far. It makes me chuckle; it almost reads like a diversity parody. In one of the shared apartments toward the back of the building lives Rahel, a part-Kenyan, part-Swiss lesbian. The largest apartment in the building is rented by an Orthodox Jewish couple with five children. Every Friday they put a sticker over the light sensor in the hallway to stop the light from coming on during the Sabbath. Then there is Tato, the gay Brazilian masseur. His friend Pablo, the Spanish fashion designer, lives in a shared apartment right next to Olivier and Ruth—he's a French insurance expert, she's a German therapist. Then there's Frederike, the middle-class cellist, and her neighbor from the countryside, Silvia, who uses a wheelchair. And a few doors down there's Klaus, an electrician with East German roots, whom Silvia has labeled "the phantom" because he rarely shows his face. Seventy-nine percent of the Swiss population are Swiss citizens. At Kalkbreite, that share is 75 percent.[2] In Switzerland, 31 percent of the population have an annual income of between forty thousand and sixty thousand Swiss francs (about $42,000–$62,000). At Kalkbreite, that figure is 29 percent.[3] In some respects it seems that Kalkbreite has indeed managed to recreate a mini-Switzerland, but not in every aspect. The residents here are younger, they are better educated, and there are more women than the national average. The difference isn't massive, but it's there. The homogenization processes that lead to social segregation in large cities are slowed down somewhat. Consequently, segregation is less pronounced at Kalkbreite, but even here it's not possible to stop it altogether, as is demonstrated by an event that took place in the fall of 2015.

A room even smaller than Silvia's was becoming available in Cluster One. The overall makeup of the Kalkbreite population at the time was already a little too much on the young, foreign, female, and well-educated side, so the room should have been allocated to a Swiss man over fifty without a university degree—to a skilled worker, maybe; there weren't many of them at Kalkbreite.

One Tuesday evening, a residents' meeting was convened. Around fifty people had gathered in the cafeteria; Silvia was sitting at the back. When they got to the issue of the imminent vacancy, she saw Fred get up and walk to the front. Fred Frohofer, a slim man in his mid-fifties with fine features and a soft voice, lived in the room opposite the one that was becoming available. He announced that they wanted to take in a refugee. At the time, hundreds of thousands of refugees were coming to Europe. Most were heading for Germany, but many were arriving in Switzerland too. Fred and the other residents of Cluster One wanted to set an example. "It had never occurred to me that anyone might object," he told me later.

When Fred had finished, Silvia raised her hand. Why should such a beautiful, low-priced room be given to a foreigner just like that, she asked. Did they not know how long wheelchair users had to wait for this type of apartment? And, she added, would someone who's fled from a war zone not need a lot of help and support from their neighbors? She was not able to provide that sort of assistance, she said.

Fred had observed a lot of nodding and smiling as he spoke, but now Silvia was not the only one who voiced concerns. Since all decisions had to be agreed to unanimously, he did not put his proposition to a vote. Instead, he and his cluster neighbors found another, quieter solution. The woman who was moving out was going to sublet the room for a year—to a refugee. Nobody could object to that. And so, in place of the hypothetical Swiss man who should have moved in, an Afghan woman joined Cluster One: Jamila Hadi, fifty-five, from Kabul.

On the morning of December 6, 2015, Silvia made her way to the canteen kitchen on the first floor, where a chef usually prepared dinner in the evenings. Today, however, there was a potluck brunch to celebrate the Feast of St. Nicholas, and Silvia had baked a braided bread. That was when she first saw Jamila. Jamila was wearing a knitted pink cardigan and had brought something that looked like rice pudding but turned out to be a sweet Afghan dish with sugar, pistachios, and cardamom. It was delicious. They exchanged a few words—Silvia can't remember what they spoke about exactly but recalls that she enjoyed their brief conversation. She had expected to find a traumatized person, but Jamila struck her as determined and certainly not in need of assistance.

Silvia didn't work because she was no longer able to; Jamila didn't because she wasn't yet allowed to. They both had time on their hands, and so they began to visit each other. Sometimes they'd eat together or go to Pablo's sewing class in the cafeteria. Silvia had a Swiss Rail travel card, and one day, as she was leaving for a day trip to Lake Geneva, she bumped into Jamila at the streetcar stop outside the house. Jamila mentioned that she'd love to go there too, one day. As a wheelchair user, Silvia was entitled to take along a companion free of charge. On her next trip, Jamila joined her. In the winter, they hopped on a train to escape the gray fog of the city and headed for the clean, clear mountain air of the Grisons. The snow lay several feet deep, and the temperature was well below freezing, but they sat outside anyway, warmed by lambskins, the alpine sun, and hot punch. They traveled to the official opening of the new Gotthard Base Tunnel, the world's longest rail tunnel. Silvia explained the word *Jahrhundertprojekt*, project of the century, to Jamila, and Jamila teased Silvia for falling asleep in the middle of a fairground while Jamila was tossing balls at a row of coconuts, winning herself a handbag. Silvia showed Jamila around Switzerland, and in turn Jamila did Silvia's laundry and cooked for her. By now, Silvia's new favorite dish was Kabuli palaw, an Afghan rice dish with carrots, raisins, and lamb.

Jamila Hadi's story is more than just another example of the power of contact. It also demonstrates just how resistant human nature is to this kind of contact. The Kalkbreite residents had agreed on a quota system to foster diversity. But in a situation that the quotas were ultimately designed for, Silvia would have preferred another wheelchair user, and Fred would have preferred a refugee. On one thing, they both agreed: Just this once, it would be okay to flout the rules.

Just this once—that's a phrase often heard at Kalkbreite. The human longing for kindred spirits is driving the relentless search for new ways to squeeze more homogeneity into the building. The shared apartments are the main gateways.

Whenever a room becomes available, it is the roommates who decide who gets to move in, changing the demographic fabric of the entire complex in the process. The largest shared apartment has seventeen bedrooms and is aptly named *Murmelibau*, groundhog burrow. When I knock on the door, I meet Markus, a landscape architect in his late forties, wearing glasses and a turtleneck sweater. As he shows me around, he lists his roommates' occupations: another architect, a social worker, another—no, two more social workers, a caregiver, and a nursery teacher—overall predominantly social jobs, he says. Two floors above, three psychology students, university friends, are sharing an apartment with an economics student of the same age.

An employee at the management office tells me, "Staying within the social mixing rules is a nightmare."

Considering that assessment, it does work astonishingly well, though, at least as far as the five criteria of the leasing regulations are concerned. In one area, however, it fails miserably: political beliefs.

In the National Council, the lower house of the Swiss parliament, the right-wing populist SVP party is the largest faction by far, with sixty-five out of two hundred seats (in 2016). At Kalkbreite, I can't find a single person who supports them, let alone voted for them. The people here are left-wing through and through. Even those from a conservative background such as Frederike, the cellist, have gradually edged closer to the left. I have not heard of any political conflicts at Kalkbreite—except maybe the battle over the poster in the purple stairwell.

Fred Frohofer and the other members of the simple-living initiative *Leicht Leben*—which aims to raise environmental awareness among the Kalkbreite residents—have designed posters on a number of green issues. There's one about water consumption, one about electrosmog, and another about air pollution. And there is one that explains that switching to green electricity would cost residents less than a chocolate bar per month.

One day, the members of the *Leicht Leben* group put up posters in each of Kalkbreite's seven stairwells, which are each painted a different color. The following day, Fred noticed that the one in the purple stairwell had been reversed so that it was facing the wall. Fred hung it the right way around. The next day, it had been flipped over again. Fred hung it the right way around again. The next morning, it was facing the wall again. He swapped it for a different poster, but it made no difference. He tried all the other designs, but each time, the poster was reversed the next day. There were no issues in any of the other stairwells.

Fred stuck a note next to the poster, inviting a conversation. No one came forward. Then he wrote a personal message to the offender on the back of the poster. The next day, it was revealed for all to see.

Fred put up a clip frame, displaying the poster behind glass. The next morning, it was reversed again. Whoever had done it must have carefully removed the glass, flipped the poster over, and then reinserted it into the frame without breaking it.

Fred was not someone who gave up easily. He inserted two screws into the frame, one on each side. The environment is important to Fred. He is a vegan and works for Greenpeace; he wears only secondhand clothes and hardly ever flies, but his nemesis must have had an Allen wrench.

In the fall of 2018, after forty or so silent battles, Fred decided on a different approach. He hung up a poster condemning the self-determination initiative, a referendum introduced by the SVP. Its opponents, Fred and everyone else I met at Kalkbreite included, feared that if it were adopted, the initiative would enable the government to withdraw from important international treaties. When Fred came to check on the poster the next day, it was still hanging the right way around. It remained so until November, when the initiative was quashed by a majority of the Swiss voters. Fred took the poster down and refrained from replacing it with a *Leicht Leben* one. His adversary had won. But who was it?

The first name I hear suggested is Klaus, so I thought I'd have a chat with him. I walk up to his apartment, but as I'm about to twist the usual golden bell at his door, I find it has been removed. In its place there is a small black notebook and a sharp, untouched pencil. I check the Kalkbreite phone directory, but there's no phone number listed for him and no email address. I knock on his door, but there's no answer. I try again a few more times with no luck. I drop a letter in his mailbox, but again, nothing.

At this point, I have spoken with around three dozen Kalkbreite residents. Even the Jewish family, whom people had described to me as very reclusive, welcomed me into their apartment. All agreed to talk, except Klaus. But I'm not the only one he doesn't speak to. Officially, he's part of Silvia's cluster, but they haven't seen him for a long time. I can't find anyone who knows him well. Ostensibly, he's not interested in contact with others. That's okay; after all, there can't be any obligation to meet others, even in a building that is designed to facilitate contact. They must all respect it, and most of Klaus's neighbors do. In fact, I am rather delighted by how undogmatic the residents generally are. Kalkbreite doesn't feel so much like a commune, more like a marketplace that people are free to enter or not as they please. And Klaus has chosen not to enter it.

The only reason I bring him up is because his case highlights the price we pay for seclusion. Of all the residents at Kalkbreite, Klaus (whose name I have changed) seems to be the one who has distanced himself the most from his neighbors. By doing so, he has created room for prejudice and preconceptions. Someone told me Klaus was right-wing, another said he was a left-wing extremist. A third thought he was a radical eco-warrior. I hear he's a drinker, a rebel, an intellectual. People say that he's tight-fisted, bookish, chasing a woman who's young enough to be his daughter.

It takes me a while to realize why these rumors seem so bizarre to me; after all, they're just ordinary gossip. Then I get it: that's the point; here, that's not ordinary. To the contrary. I have encountered very little bias at Kalkbreite. Maybe it's because the people here tend to talk with each other rather than about each other. Klaus is the exception.

All the apartment doors at Kalkbreite are the same, even Klaus's, but they all look different. They are all made of heavy, light-colored wood, with bells mounted at hip height. However, most residents have personalized their front doors. Silvia has hung a picture on her door of Malala Yousafzai, the Pakistani Nobel Peace Prize laureate; Frederike has a sign identifying herself as a cellist, and photos from a holiday in Tunisia. Other doors are adorned with children's paintings, a photo of the Earth, or a Chinese movie poster. The residents use their front doors like store windows, giving clues to who lives inside.

Klaus too has personalized his entrance. He hasn't hung anything on his door, but there's a sticker on the shoe cabinet next to it that shows a cormorant, with the words "Bird of the Year 2010." A second sticker shows a nuthatch, "Bird of the Year 2006." A third has a picture of an empty battery next to the words "Nature's resources."

Of all the allegations I have heard about him, radical eco-warrior therefore seems the most likely to be true. I don't believe that he was the offender of the purple stairway. Why would someone who obviously cares about nature reverse posters proposing a switch to green energy? Of course, this is merely another allegation, a prejudice that I can neither confirm nor refute without speaking to Klaus. On the day of my departure, before I leave for the station, I scribble a few of these thoughts in the notebook by Klaus's door. It's the first entry, and it fills seventeen pages. Three days later, I receive a typewritten reply.

"Of what I was being accused of, I had no idea," Klaus writes. "Some may see indeed something rebellious in reversing posters. That is of no concern to me. The building is teeming with social workers and psychologists, so one might have expected a little more understanding for an apparent oddball. What say you? Is that a positive prejudice toward these occupations?" Now I know that he's smart, and probably well read. Before he concludes his letter with a handwritten "Moin, Moin!"—a friendly and informal greeting that is used in Hamburg where I live—he comments on a sentence I wrote in his notebook, "Prejudice grows where people don't know each other, where there is distance between them."

Klaus replies: "Your theory seems insufficiently complex to me. It doesn't explain why long-standing neighbors in the

Balkan Wars of the 1990s started to rob, rape, and slaughter one another. Those people worked side by side in the same public enterprises, and their children went to the same schools."

Reading this, I regret not having written another seventeen pages in his notebook, because Klaus is right, of course. His argument holds up a massive "but" to the contact hypothesis. It's not only in the Balkans that people betrayed their friends. In Rwanda too, people massacred their neighbors. There are stories from almost every war in history of people who knew each other well, yet acted upon prejudice as if they were strangers, stories of people who were unaffected by contact, unprotected against hatred and animosity, and unmoved by empathy. How can that be explained?

The answer will become clear in the next chapter and will lead directly to the answer to another question. Can the power of contact that developed between Michael Kent and Tiffany Whittier, between Christa and Harald Hermes and their Serbs, the same power that Thorleif Link used specifically to deter Jamal from becoming a terrorist, that changed Finbarr O'Brien's and Chris Lyons's lives and by extension those of the Irish in general, that made friends out of neighbors at Kalkbreite, be employed on a larger scale to help reconcile entire societies, even those that are deeply divided? In short: Yes, it can. There is a society where this has happened, which to this day has utilized the tool of contact as radically and extensively as likely no other in the world. That society will be the subject of the last chapter, but first, Klaus gets his response.

The Community

How contact can lead to war

One of the most famous social psychology experiments
dates back to the summer of 1954.[1] Psychologists in Oklahoma selected twenty-two fifth graders who didn't know each
other but who shared several common characteristics. They
were all male, White, Protestant, middle class, and achieved
roughly the same grades at school. Eleven of them were sent to
one summer camp, the other eleven to a different camp nearby.

After a week, the psychologists organized a sports tournament that included baseball and tug-of-war. The teams chose
names for themselves: the Eagles and the Rattlers. Even before
the first competition had begun, the teams started hurling abuse
at each other. After a couple of days, the Eagles burned the Rattlers' flag. In retaliation, the Rattlers raided the Eagles' quarters
and stole their captain's jeans as a replacement. The Eagles took
their revenge by entering their opponents' camp and muddying
their beds. They retreated to their own camp and stuffed socks
with stones to use as weapons. When a fistfight broke out, the
psychologists stopped the experiment.

The boys had formed two tribes within a week. The individual no longer mattered; there was only *us* and *them*. Their group identities were so strong that the boys used violence against other boys who objectively were no less like them than the boys on their own team. Contact with the others had not led to empathy, but to war.

Reading about the experiment, the British social psychologist Henri Tajfel wondered: At what point exactly did the animosity set in? At the start, all the boys were the same. By the end, they had become enemies. When did the differences displace the similarities? He designed his own experiment to find out.[2]

Tajfel also began with people who were similar: students from the University of Bristol, where he worked. One by one, he invited them to his office and assigned them to one of two groups. Using a variety of systems—for example by flipping a coin in front of their eyes—he made sure that they saw that the allocation was totally random and that there was no material distinction between the groups.

Tajfel planned to then introduce subtle differences. One group, for example, would start wearing hats while the other wouldn't, and so on. With every added difference, the group identities would become more pronounced. When would the first group begin to see the second group no longer just as people but as "the others"? At what point would tribal thinking kick in?

Before he began, he asked each student, "While you're here, would you mind helping me out with a second, totally unrelated experiment?" The students were asked to divide some money between two groups, one of which just so happened to have the same name as the one they had just been assigned to. Tajfel expected that the students would not display a preference for either group. Why would they? This was an independent experiment. What is more, they had been alone in the room since they had heard about their own group allocation. They didn't know any of the members of their own group or of the other. There was absolutely no shared identity, no shared experience, not a single shared second, and nothing that would define the group except for its name, which for all intents and purposes had been chosen at random. And yet, when it came to allocating the money, the students systematically preferred their "own" group.

It didn't need a sports tournament; it didn't need any hats. The flip of a coin was sufficient to kickstart tribal thinking. Since then, social psychologists have proved with countless further experiments that humans develop group identities over the most trivial factors. We just can't help ourselves.

By itself, this wouldn't be so bad if it weren't for two effects that go hand in hand with the phenomenon, both of which manifested themselves in the Oklahoma experiment. First, people in groups lose sight of reality. Apart from baseball and tug-of-war, the Eagles and Rattlers also competed at collecting beans. Each boy would give their yield to the experiment leader, who would then pretend to tip them onto the plate of an overhead projector. The boys from both teams would therefore be able to see the beans that had been collected. In reality, however, the leader would pour a specific number of beans onto the plate—the same for each boy. Each time, he asked the boys to guess how many beans there were, and each time, the boys overestimated the performance of their own teammates and underestimated that of the other's. It is likely this happened at a subconscious level.

In addition, the psychologists had observed the Eagles boasting among themselves about how they had scared away the Rattlers, even though it wasn't true. Separately, they observed the Rattlers convincing each other that the Eagles had dumped garbage on their beach. In reality, they had left it there themselves the night before. In each case, the teams, or at least some of their members, must have been aware of the truth, but it didn't matter. They lied and twisted reality until it served the us-versus-them narrative. Their perception had become tribalized.

The November 1951 game between Princeton and Dartmouth was one of the most brutal meets in college football. In the second quarter, a star player from Princeton left the field with a broken nose. In the third quarter, a Dartmouth player broke his leg. There were few moves that didn't involve a foul. In the aftermath, Dartmouth blamed Princeton for the violence, and vice versa.

A few weeks later, social psychologists played video footage of the match in lecture halls at both universities and asked the students to fill out a questionnaire. The Princeton students counted twice as many fouls as the Dartmouth students. They calculated the ratio of severe to light fouls as two to one. The Dartmouth students made it one to one. At Princeton, 86 percent of the students said that Dartmouth had started the violence; at Dartmouth only 36 percent agreed.[3]

The students at the two universities had seen the same footage of the same game with the same specifics but drew completely different conclusions. Loyalty to their own team was more important to them than getting the facts right. They acted tribally.

Arguably, football may not be best suited to such an experiment because the events on the field are often open to interpretation. The same cannot be said, however, about an experiment carried out by the social psychologist Solomon Asch that same year.[4] Asch showed each of his participants a piece of paper with a line on it. Then he showed them another piece of paper with three lines on it: one exactly the same length as the first, one much longer, and one much shorter. In more than 99 percent of the cases, the participants correctly identified the line of the same length. It was a very easy task.

Then Asch altered the experiment. He introduced six extra people into the room who—unbeknownst to the participant— were part of the experiment setup. The examiner first asked the six new people in the room, one after the other, which line was the same length as the first one. Because they were in on it, all six gave the same—wrong—answer. The actual participant was asked last. In 37 percent of cases, the participant also gave the wrong answer, even though they must have known perfectly well that it wasn't true. Like the students at Princeton and Dartmouth, they opted for loyalty to the group over truthfulness.

Since then, social scientists have been able to manipulate people in all sorts of ways. For example, they convinced Democrats to support a Republican social policy by pretending that it was endorsed by their own party. It worked the other way around too, with views on climate change or gun laws; the result was always the same. No matter what the issue is, people like to stick to their team. This blind loyalty can be very risky, even more so considering the second effect of group formation, as witnessed in the Oklahoma experiment: aggression between Eagles and Rattlers was not the exception but the rule.

Scientists have established the link between group identity and aggression against outsiders right down to our biology. When we see a picture of a sad person from within our group, we feel sad too. If it's someone from a rival group, we feel glad.[5] When we see a member of our own group being stabbed in the hand with a needle, we feel pain. If it's a member of a different group, it doesn't bother us. In certain circumstances it can even delight us: MRIs have shown that such images activate the reward center in our brain.[6]

When we feel threatened in our group identity—when we hear a racist slur, for example—our body produces increased levels of the stress hormone cortisol, which can be detected in our saliva. Our body's response is the same as if we had encountered a wolf in the woods. We get ready to fight, and we stop seeing members of the other camp primarily as human beings; they become our enemies.[7]

This is what happened during the Balkan Wars of the 1990s when old friends turned on each other. As members of a group, their systems were flushed with cortisol. The same thing happened in Rwanda, where Hutus took to attacking their Tutsi neighbors with machetes. And that's what's happening today when refugee hostels and the cars of right-wing politicians are set on fire, and when people drive their cars into demonstrators or attack the offices of elected officials. The cortisol levels of many people in Western societies are on the rise.

This raises a new question: Harald Hermes, Sven Krüger, Jamal, and Finbarr O'Brien all felt threatened in their group identities when they met their enemies. Why did contact for them eventually lead to empathy and friendship and not, as with the Eagles and the Rattlers, to hatred and violence?

In each of these previous cases they met their enemies alone—in a living room, a prison gym, a police station, or a hotel bar. Their meetings took place away from the arena of tribal wars. If a lone Eagle and a lone Rattler had bumped into one another in the woods, away from the main camp, it's likely they would not have gotten into a fight. They might even have discovered that they liked each other and become friends. But they didn't encounter each other in that way. Instead, they were standing together with their teammates on a baseball field or pulling on the same rope with them. The Princeton students were sitting next to other Princeton students in a Princeton lecture hall. The man who drove his car into a crowd of counterprotesters in Charlottesville in 2017, killing a young woman, also felt that he belonged to a group; he was surrounded by thousands of people from both camps.

The Scottish neuroscientist Ian Robertson studied these kinds of intense group situations by looking at terrorists in particular. "When people bond together, oxytocin levels rise in their blood," Robertson writes.[8] Oxytocin is the human bonding hormone, and it acts at the mammary glands of lactating mothers to induce milk to be produced for the baby. Like a natural drug, it causes a high. It is released during intense group situations like tug-of-war or amid a crowd of protestors confronted with a group of angry counterprotesters. Its job is to make the individual feel bonded to their group like a baby to its mother.

Together with testosterone, the dominance hormone, which is released at the same time in these situations, they create a biochemical high more powerful than cocaine or alcohol, Robertson writes. "It makes it easier for you to anesthetize your empathy for the out-group and to see them as objects." It explains why groups are capable of savagery, much more so than any individual alone.[9]

Klaus from Kalkbreite was right. Sometimes empathy doesn't stand a chance, as when it is numbed by powerful group identities. Sometimes contact is counterproductive: when people are not meeting as individuals but as groups, as tribes.

This phenomenon is currently occurring in many places, but nowhere more so than in America. At a press conference shortly before the end of his second term, President Barack Obama cautioned against "tribalism."[10] Just a few years earlier, one might have wondered what on earth he was talking about. But Obama was right, of course. The country has split into two tribes.

The sociologist Arlie Russell Hochschild describes these two tribes in her book *Strangers in Their Own Land*.[11] One tribe is the blue, liberal America. Its people live on the coasts and in the cities, read *The New York Times*, eat organic food, separate their recycling, travel to work by bike or public transportation, and are more likely to have a college degree. The other tribe is the red, conservative America. They live in the country, watch Fox News, drive big cars, like their food deep-fried, and are on average poorer, fatter, sicker, and less well educated. They even favor different dog breeds, Hochschild writes. Liberals like Labradors, while conservatives prefer bulldogs.[12]

In Oklahoma, eleven Eagles and eleven Rattlers were pitted against each other, carefully supervised by adults ready to intervene. Today, there are millions of Labradors and millions of Bulldogs, and there is no one to stop the experiment. Only they themselves can stop it.

There is some good news. Just as tribal thinking is the natural enemy of empathy, empathy is the natural enemy of tribal thinking. All that's needed for empathy to prevail is for enough Labradors and Bulldogs to step out of their tribal formations and meet in person, at the individual level, outside of politics, in gyms, hotel bars, and living rooms. Easier said than done?

• • •

Sean Murphy* and Laura Messing have never met, but they have much in common. They are both in their early thirties and live in New York City. Both consider themselves nonpolitical but became deeply politicized by the 2016 election of Donald Trump. Both assert that the protection of minorities is the most important political virtue for them—not just in principle, but also because they have a personal stake in it. Sean Murphy is gay; Laura Messing is Jewish.

The day after the election, Sean canceled the yoga class he was going to teach and instead wandered through the streets of Brooklyn with a neighbor. Mostly they walked in silence; sometimes they cried.

Laura went to the campus of Columbia University, where she was studying psychology, but broke down in tears in a bathroom stall. For the first time in her life, she remembers, she felt

---

* Not his real name.

political hatred. *Those selfish human-hating imbeciles who had made this man president!*

The day after the inauguration, Sean and Laura both joined the Women's March in New York City, two tiny particles in a political mass of millions of like-minded people, two members of a tribal assembly. Both soon realized, however, that there was little point in talking only with people who felt just as they did. They resolved to talk to people on the other side, ideally one to one, calmly, and to convince them that they were wrong. In January 2017, Sean and Laura stood at the same starting point, and with the same goal.

Three months later, in April 2017, I meet up with Sean and ask him how many Trump voters he has talked to. None, he says. His partner, his friends, his neighbors and acquaintances, his yoga students, the journalists whose articles he reads, and even his elected representatives, whom he calls from time to time to vent his anger—they're all members of his tribe. Wherever he turns, he is met with further affirmation of his beliefs. Where would he begin anyway? He doesn't know any Trump voters apart from his father, and they aren't in touch because he wouldn't accept Sean's homosexuality.

When Laura found herself crying in the bathroom after the election, she scared herself. "On the one hand, I felt this deep hatred toward everyone who had voted for him. I thought they were misanthropic morons like him. On the other hand, I knew that was irrational. After all, I didn't know a single Trump supporter," she said. At the time, Laura was studying a course in conflict resolution and mediation, and she had learned that people who feel threatened tend to oversimplify and hypersterotype the other. She also knew that all this achieves is to make things worse, and now she observed this response in herself. "There was this interesting dichotomy within me, and I wanted to resolve it."

Laura gathered her closest friends in her small New York apartment and asked them if they knew any conservatives. No one did. She wrote an email to the New York branch of the Young Republicans, suggesting a dinner party, "four of you, four of us."

"I thought those idiots would never reply anyway," she says. A few days later someone named Samantha replied: "Good idea; we'd love to."

One Saturday evening in April, Laura and three of her liberal friends gathered in her apartment and waited. Laura had borrowed a long table and a few chairs, had bought flowers and pizza dough, and had written place cards and prepared questions. The red wine was breathing, the beer was chilled, but the Republicans were missing. "They won't come," her friends said.

"They will; believe me," insisted Laura. She had spoken on the phone with Samantha, and with a man named Roger. Both had seemed nice.

They came. Samantha, Roger, an Asian-looking woman who introduced herself as Alli, and a brawny Black guy named Joe. Laura was surprised—a Black man and an Asian woman, Republicans? The group stood around awkwardly in the kitchen, but the wine helped. Everyone added their favorite toppings to their pizza, and Laura baked them, one after the other, in her tiny oven. After a while the room filled with smoke and the smoke alarm went off. Amid the deafening noise, everything was suddenly happening at once. One person jumped on a chair, another held their legs, a third passed a towel to fan away the smoke, and a fourth opened the window. Once calm had been restored, they looked at each other and laughed at their first nonpartisan act of the evening. "It was a really serendipitous moment that we couldn't have planned but was kind of the soul of what I was trying to do," Laura tells me.

In the summer, Sean and his partner—newly wed—flew to Italy for their honeymoon. In a café in Florence, an elderly American couple sat down next to them and started talking among themselves. Sean heard the words "lying press" and became incensed. *They've got to be Trump voters*, he thought. Of all the places he could have had that conversation, it had to be the other end of the world. *But not on my honeymoon*, he later remembers thinking. He and his husband got up and left. Trump had been in office for six months, and Sean still had not had a single exchange with a fan of the president.

Around the same time, the second dinner party was underway, this time at Roger's: a barbecue in the garden with ten people. Laura had organized it together with Roger, and Alli had helped too. Sometimes they met for coffee, sometimes for dinner, and once Alli's children had joined them. "I learned a very simple fact that was actually a revelation for me," Laura says. "Nothing bad happens when you get along with someone from the other side. I always had it that it made you a traitor. But then I realized, no bombs go off, you don't die, and you don't turn into a toad. You're still the same person, except a little wiser."

Laura had managed to say, *No, that line is not the same length as the first; the six of you are wrong; it's this one; have a closer look here*. She opted against loyalty to her team and for truthfulness instead.

By November 2017, a year after the election, Sean still had not spoken to a single Trump voter. Laura, however, had organized six dinner parties. She had created a website and come up with a name, "Experiment in Dialogue." She had raised funds and found locations, together with Samantha—or Sam, as she called her now—but above all, with Roger and Alli, who had become close friends of hers. At the dinner parties, she had talked with many conservatives, and one young woman had even told her that she wouldn't vote for Trump again.

It really had been quite simple—all it took was to eat together. But how difficult that had been, considering all the things that had to come together. Laura had to be wise and self-aware enough not to follow her hatred but to recognize how irrational it was. The situation was helped by the fact that she was in a course at one of the best universities in the country that taught exactly what she needed to solve the problem that she found herself in. She had to have the guts to reach out to the other side. She had to have the time to organize it all—luckily her job wasn't very demanding, so she could do this at work. Lying awake the night before the first dinner party, she had to push away the thought that it was a really, really stupid idea to invite these people into her apartment. And finally, she had to spend a few hundred dollars on food and drinks. Who does that sort of thing? Who is able to? Most people probably choose the same path as Sean Murphy, Labradors and Bulldogs alike.

Laura Messing has not changed her political attitudes. Like Sean, she still supports the protection of minorities. Like Sean, she condemns Trump's gaffes. And like him, she cried after Charlottesville. Were they to meet, they'd probably get along great. But unlike Sean, Laura has given up her tribal identity. No longer a Labrador, she has joined a new tribe, a small tribe at the center, whose members now also include—thanks to Laura—Sam, Roger, and Alli. It's a tribe that is distinguished by the fact that its members are free to have different political opinions and still like each other as human beings.

They've started a new group. Now all this group needs to do is grow, so much so that it catches up with the other two groups, and eventually swallows them up until it is the only one left. This is exactly what happened in another country, at the other end of the world.

The Letters

Where contact has brought peace
to an entire society

In the tech world, there is a rule: Only one out of ten start-ups will succeed; the other nine will fail. The rule seems to apply to Africa too. In the 1960s, in a wave of decolonization, dozens of countries started on the road to independence. Many expected wealth and development to ensue, but most erupted into violence instead. Many people died, economies suffered, and infrastructures crumbled. One country, however, fulfilled the expectations: Botswana.

In the three decades following its independence, in 1966, Botswana's economy grew faster than that of the United States, Germany, or China—faster, in fact, than any other country in the world. To start with, there were just under ten miles of paved roads in this sub-Saharan country. Today, there are more than ten thousand. In 1966, Botswana didn't even have a capital city because its British colonial masters had ruled the country from neighboring South Africa. Today, gleaming shopping malls adorn the center of Gaborone, a city with a population of nearly a quarter of a million people, where once there was nothing but dry savanna. In 1966, only twenty-two people in the entire country had a college degree; today, highly educated Batswana are ubiquitous. The older generations went to South Africa, America, the UK, or Sweden to study, since there were no universities in the country. After they graduated, however, they returned to their home country and built government buildings, hospitals, universities, and airports. They built power lines and waterpipes across the vast plains, and it would soon strike younger generations, who were born during this boom phase, as odd that there should still be places in the country where instant access to electricity and running water are not a given.

For the citizens of Botswana, education is largely free, from nursery school through college. Every year thousands of young Batswana attend college. Most stay in the country, but many go abroad to study, including at top schools such as Harvard or Oxford—with tuition, plane tickets, and accommodation costs all covered by the government. Visits to the doctor are free too, as are seeds, fertilizer, and harvest hands. According to Transparency International, Botswana is not just the least corrupt country in Africa, it is also less corrupt than some European countries such as Italy, Spain, or Malta.[1] And while other African nations are being controlled by doddering dictators, Botswanan newspapers complain that their president has missed the gender equality goal of a balanced cabinet. How was this possible, especially given the starting conditions?

Like many other African nations, Botswana had been ruled by the British Empire. Its borders were drawn with a brutally straight pencil line in some London office. As a result, tribes that longed to be together were torn apart and others that were reluctant to live side by side were confined together. Additionally, like in other African countries, there are vast riches buried in Botswana's soil—diamonds, to be precise, which rival tribes might well have been motivated to fight over.

Elsewhere, new nation-states on the continent began to disintegrate after independence: in Nigeria, it didn't take long for the Igbo and the Yoruba to take up arms. In the Congo, the Katanga and Kasai provinces broke away, sinking the 250 ethnic groups in the country into a bloody civil war. In Mali, the Tuareg started an uprising. But in Botswana, relations between the roughly two dozen tribes remained peaceful. While, much later, in Rwanda, the Hutu committed genocide against the Tutsi, and Sierra Leone descended into a tribal war fueled by diamonds, the Botswanan tribes were merging into one nation.

Traveling through the country in 2018, I spoke with dozens of Batswana about their identity. Not one of them mentioned their tribe without being asked. Fifty years ago, that would have been unthinkable, people tell me. Now, they call themselves city folk, global citizens, feminists, Africans, but mostly they start by saying, "I'm Motswana." This country is likely the most successful example of nation-building in the history of nations. It was able to bring together a mixed society made up of multiple ethnic groups, numerous languages, and sometimes hostile tribes to form a single unit.

• • •

One day in March 2004, Carol Ramolotsana, a religious-education teacher, was called to the principal's office at the school where she worked. He handed her a large white envelope with the stamp of the Ministry of Basic Education. She immediately knew it meant a transfer and wondered, *Where to?* In Botswana, teachers are civil servants assigned to a school by the government. Carol opened the envelope and read "Lentsweletau," Lion Hill. She had never heard of the place, and in Botswana that means only one thing: It's a one-horse town. Carol sank into the chair opposite the principal's desk and started to cry. She says she will never forget the emptiness, the speechlessness she felt in that moment. Back at home, she looked at a map of her country. Wedged between South Africa to the south, Namibia to the north and west, and Zimbabwe to the east, Botswana is larger than California, but its population is smaller than that of Chicago. Carol moved her finger across the map and stopped at a small dot on the edge of the Kalahari Desert. Lentsweletau, with a population of five thousand, was in Kweneng district, home to the Bakwena tribe, known for worshipping crocodiles.

That's where she was to live? She, a city girl, was to be a teacher at a village school?

As a civil servant, Carol had been aware of the risk of transfer, but, she says, it had seemed as unreal to her as catching a deadly disease seems to a healthy young person, like something that only ever happens to other people. Moments earlier, she had been a happy twenty-nine-year-old woman who enjoyed her life in the capital, going out to the movies or getting sweet and sour chicken at her favorite Chinese restaurant. She was a regular at O'Hagan's Irish pub, where a friend of hers sang African soul music. She had just started a postgraduate education course for which she had saved up for a long time, 6,600 pula, or $560 US. *And*, she remembers thinking angrily, *that was all over because someone at the Ministry of Basic Education had said so?*

She wrote to the Ministry to complain. She went there in person, but to no avail. A few days later, a truck stopped in front of her house at the school where she had worked. In Botswana, schoolteachers commonly live on campus, in state-subsidized housing. The movers, hired by the government, carried box after box out of her home. Her sofa, her fridge, her bed—her whole life disappeared into the truck. Then it rumbled off in the direction of the Kalahari Desert, leaving her behind in the city that she loved, alone in her empty apartment.

That night, she slept on her sister's couch, and the next, and the one after that. Eventually, someone from the ministry called and told her that if she didn't show up for work at her new school soon, she would be dismissed. The following morning, she got into her Honda Civic and headed for Lentsweletau.

Just like Carol, Bakang Nkwe, an elementary school teacher, had never heard of the place that the ministry had chosen for him. For quite a while he stood in the principal's office of his school, searching the map on the wall. When he'd finally found the place, his head was tilted all the way back. Nokaneng, population fifteen hundred, is right up north where the mighty Okavango River disappears into the sands of the Kalahari Desert, forming the largest inland river delta on the planet. It was in the northwest district, home of the Herero, a tribe about whom Bakang knew almost nothing at all.

Bakang was twenty-four, born in the South, and had never left his region. He was at home here, had gone to college, played for the national softball team. Here he had met his girlfriend, to whom he had just proposed, but now there was no time to get married.

He boarded the bus headed north. A two-day trip, seven hundred and fifty miles, separating the world he loved and the world he feared, his present and his future. His friends had intimated that up north they had no electricity or running water, and that the people were as wild as the animals. They warned him to be careful, lest he be eaten by a lion or trampled to death by an elephant.

It was the middle of the night when the bus dropped him off at the side of a deserted road. In the dark, on his way to the school on the outskirts of the village, Bakang thought he saw a silhouette of a man with two horns on his massive head.

Carol steered her car out of the city, the sparkling towers of Gaborone disappearing in her rearview mirror. The roads narrowed, the landscape widened. By the side of the road, simple dwellings crouched under a huge sky; all around was pale yellow savanna. The first things she saw of Lentsweletau were a crumbling ruin on the left side of the road and a half-finished gas station on the right: no movie theaters, no clubs, no Chinese restaurants.

The school consisted of a few dozen huts generously dotted over the red earth. In between, a few trees provided shade against the sun, which even at the end of summer was still beating down mercilessly. She went to the secretary's office and collected the key for No. 24, the small brick house that was to be her new home. She remembers sitting down on the bed, weeping.

Over the following days, she heard the children clamoring outside. Carol stayed in bed and ignored anyone who came to her door. She had brought a sack of rice, some pasta, corn flour, ten pounds of dried chicken, and enough cider to last a while. It was several days before she put on her high heels, clutched her handbag, and walked to her lessons. Her colleagues laughed. "What a fine lady," teased one. "You'll leave those high-heeled shoes eventually," remarked another.

They were exactly how Carol had imagined village people to be, with short hair, flat worn-out shoes, and no handbags. She was convinced many of them didn't shower.

Carol spent her lunchtimes alone in her house. After lessons were over, she cracked open her first can of Hunter's apple cider, 4.9 percent alcohol. She had brought it from Gaborone.

She used to love teaching. She had wanted to be a teacher since sixth grade, she remembers, inspired by a teacher who would sometimes bring oranges to class and comb the hair of those children whose parents didn't own a comb. Once she had become a teacher herself, she would hand out sweets to her class. In Gaborone—not here. Here, she looked at her students and saw small versions of the villagers, whom she despised. Sometimes, she would give them a book to read at the beginning of a lesson and then go back to her room to cry.

When she had finished her supply of cider, Carol drove to the village bar. She ignored the stares, and the stench of sweat and workmen's shoes. She ordered a beer at the bar and drank it outside, alone in her car. She drank five, sometimes six cans a night. Then she would drive home and go to sleep.

Bakang learned that the silhouette he had seen that first night belonged to a Herero woman wearing the traditional head-dress of her tribe. Among the thousand or so children at the elementary school where he now worked, there were many Herero. Like him, most of them lived on campus. Their villages were too far for them to walk to school every day. Bakang was supposed to teach them, but that turned out to be easier said than done. Many of them didn't speak a word of Setswana, let alone English—the official languages of Botswana, and the only ones that Bakang knew.

He felt as if he had not only traveled seven hundred and fifty miles across the desert but also fifty years into the past. There really was no electricity, and the nearest grocery store was a hundred and thirty miles away, as were the nearest bank and restaurant. The only way to "go out for a meal" was when someone in the neighborhood had slaughtered a goat or an antelope. The meat was shared with everyone.

Soon, Bakang had learned enough Herero to greet his students in their language. And soon, his students spoke enough Setswana to follow his lessons. In the evenings, he would meet up with his new buddies, some of them teachers from far away, like him. At least one evening a week, he would go on the hunt for a phone signal. If he climbed a tree or a termite mound at dusk, he might be lucky and catch one bar. More often than not, however, he would get into his 1985 VW Passat and drive for half an hour to the next village to call his girlfriend. During his time off, he would travel south to see her. It wasn't long after his second visit that she told him on the phone that she had missed her period.

He wasn't there when his daughter was born. He wasn't there when she took her first steps. Then his girlfriend broke up with him. The distance was just too great, she said.

Listening to Carol Ramolotsana and Bakang Nkwe tell me their stories in December 2018—Carol in her sister's house, where she once slept on the couch, Bakang in a hotel room in Gaborone—I can hear the resentment in their voices, even after all those years. Yes, they admit, the government must ensure that the people at Lentsweletau and in Nokaneng are able to attend school. But why, they ask, does that have to involve moving teachers from the South to the North and from the cities to the countryside? After all, there are teachers at Lentsweletau and in Nokaneng already, they argue. Teachers who, the two have learned after moving there, are sometimes sent to the South or to the cities, even though they don't want to go. They don't understand why people can't just work in their hometowns.

Botswana's Ministry for Basic Education is in a black-and-white glass building in the center of Gaborone. In his office on the second floor, Permanent Secretary Simon Coles is sitting behind a wooden desk piled high with letters, printed emails, and transcripts of phone calls. "Complaints from unhappy teachers," Coles says, gesturing at the mountain of correspondence. "Most are dismissed."

From here, it's only a three-minute walk to the Ministry of Health. They receive similar complaints, not from teachers but from doctors and nurses. Another five minutes' walk away is the Ministry of Local Government and Rural Development. They receive complaints mostly from administrative civil servants, which are equally dismissed. The Ministry of Agricultural Development receives complaints from engineers and agricultural experts. All one hundred and twenty thousand civil servants in Botswana, some 10 percent of the working population, face being transferred to a different part of the country at short notice. Whenever a health center is in need of a nurse or a hospital in need of a physician, the government will send one. Whenever a district office is short of a driver, or a town hall of a secretary, the government will send one. The nurses, doctors, drivers, and secretaries aren't asked; they're told. Many complain, but few succeed. Each week, trucks crisscross the country ferrying personal belongings from the South to the North and from the East to the West. It's not only vacancies that cause civil servants to be transferred. Teachers, for example, are expected to change posts every five years as a matter of principle, Simon Coles explains. It's one of the guidelines of the Ministry of Basic Education.

Coles and his colleagues in the other ministries had reasons for this system. But in my interviews none put it as well as Ponatshego Kedikilwe.

Kedikilwe is a man of imposing stature with a deep voice. He is wearing a brown hat against the blaring sun as he takes a seat on the veranda of his home. He was born in this village eighty years ago near the Zimbabwean border, when the British still ruled the land. In 2014, he came back here to retire. For thirty years he had been a parliamentarian, with roles as minister for trade, energy, finance, and education, chief of staff to the president, and finally vice president.

"Botswana owes its national unity to the transfer of civil servants," claims Kedikilwe. Just think back to the early of days of independence, to the summer of 1996, he adds. By the time Botswana's independence was dawning on the horizon, other African nations had already taken that step. The Congo became independent in 1960 and immediately sank into ethnic violence.

Mali also became independent in 1960, and before long the Tuareg revolted in the North.

Nigeria too became independent in 1960, and soon conflict broke out between the Igbo and the Yoruba.

It was obvious that in those places, the identities of the people did not fit the political structures; tribal loyalties did not match the new national borders and constitutions. From his own country, Prime Minister—and soon to be the first president of an independent Botswana—Seretse Khama observed how tribalism tore apart one young African nation after another. According to Kedikilwe, Khama resolved to prevent the same thing from happening in Botswana.

Yet, in his country too, tribal allegiances were strong: Each tribe had their own territory, chief, and spirit animal that was believed to say something about the tribe. For the Kalanga in the North, for example, who consider themselves good-natured, it was the elephants. For the Bakwena on the southern edge of the Kalahari, a warrior tribe, proud and uncomplicated, it was the crocodiles. There were the lions, the fish, and there was Khama's own tribe in the middle of the country, the Bangwato, the antelopes, who had formed an elite in this land since people can remember.

Khama knew that the tribal identities would have to give way to a national identity shared by all. In a sense, Seretse Khama was in a situation similar to that of Laura Messing, the young Columbia University student, half a century later. He wanted to dismantle the existing group identities and establish a new one, except that he, unlike Messing, had the political power to do so. In September 1966, he became the first president of an independent Botswana.

Maybe he had had a eureka moment, or maybe one of Khama's advisers came up with the idea of how to achieve his goal. But according to Ponatshego Kedikilwe, it seems more likely that the solution presented itself.

Khama's government had to make sure that all Batswana were able to attend school or see a doctor, even the people in the remotest regions of the country who were sustained by what they could grow themselves. They lived a life virtually unchanged for centuries. Their daily routines were governed by the rhythm of the rising and setting sun, waiting for the infrequent rain, and coping with the fierce, pitiless heat. The people were farmers; there were no teachers or doctors. So Khama's government did what the British had done before them: They sent people there. The British had sent White colonial civil servants; now it was Batswana. They may have belonged to a different tribe, but that wasn't important then—above all, they were fellow citizens. It soon emerged that these transfers had an interesting side effect.

The civil servants tasked with improving the villagers' health and education made new friends there. Some fell in love, got married, and had children. And these children suddenly had parents who came from different tribes and sometimes even spoke different languages. All over the country, in thousands of one-on-one contacts, prejudices were thrown out and new relationships formed.

Exposure, Kedikilwe says, was the key. Every citizen should be exposed to their fellow citizens, no matter which tribe they belong to, which language they speak, or where they live. In the 1940s, his parents sent him to an elementary school thirty-five miles away, Kedikilwe explains. When he arrived, he was surprised to learn that the people there weren't nearly as dumb as some in his village had claimed. One day, he overheard two schoolboys arguing. One of them claimed that trains could only travel on rails, while the other insisted that they could also travel on roads. "He just hadn't seen a train before," Kedikilwe says. "If he'd seen one, he would have known right away that he was wrong."

What Kedikilwe means is that people in tribal communities think about other tribes the way the boy thought about trains. The snakes are cunning, the crocodiles don't shower, the Herero are as wild as the animals that they share the land with. The others are the enemy.

While elsewhere in Africa stereotypes like these were fueling civil wars, Seretse Khama's government strove to dismantle them further. By the mid-seventies, they extended the transfer program for civil servants. Instead of moving them merely within their home regions, they now transferred them throughout the whole country. As a result, even more children were born with parents from different tribes. Slowly, the people were growing together. Of course, this is just one side of the story, a bird's-eye view adopted by a government observing their country. While they may have had a clear sense of the whole forest, they couldn't see the health of each individual tree.

At Lentsweletau, Carol Ramolotsana fell into depression. She only left her home to teach or drink. One Saturday in spring, five months after she had arrived, and feeling the need for a change, she left in the morning for the nearest town, about an hour's drive southeast. She sat down on a plastic chair outside the Big Six bar and had a beer. When she had nearly finished with it, a man got up and brought her another. He was tall and handsome, with broad shoulders and a big smile. He was a soldier, he told her. His name was Thabo.

Thabo asked her where she lived, and Carol replied, a little embarrassed as she now recalls, "Lentsweletau."

"What?" he replied, "that's my home village."

At the time, he lived a little farther north at an army station, but a week later he came by for a visit. He brought some friends from the village with him, who were surprised to see Carol when she opened the door. "What, this lady's your girlfriend?" they wondered. "She won't talk to anyone here."

Thabo took Carol along to a wedding party; the whole village was there. Before the event, he had bought her three skirts of the type usually worn for such occasions in the village: a blue one, a red one, and a brown one. She says he made her feel like a real lady. At the party, Thabo introduced her to many people. She didn't talk much—he did the talking for her—but she noticed that she was opening up.

Bakang also found his life changing in ways he didn't expect. When his school in Nokaneng was looking for a teacher to accompany students on a trip to the Okavango delta, he put his name forward. They boarded a small aircraft and flew over the mighty delta, Bakang in the copilot's seat. Below them, the river snaked its way through the dry land and brought the savanna to life. At night, when the children were in their beds, he sat by the river with the other guests from their lodge, admiring the moon and listening to lions roar in the distance. He had a beer, then another, and another, and asked himself why he had never visited this magical place before.

He met tourists from America, the United Kingdom, Belgium, Germany, and Japan, who paid more than a thousand dollars a night for a chance to see the Big Five animals. Bakang began to contemplate building a little house here, but his window of opportunity soon slammed shut. After two years in Nokaneng, another letter from the Ministry for Basic Education arrived. His new destination was Francistown, Central District, population one hundred thousand, the second-largest city in the country.

Bakang heaved a sigh of relief—a return to the city at last: nightlife, restaurants. He met a woman. Four years after his first daughter was born, his second daughter arrived. For a while, life was good, but then another letter came. He was ordered back to the South, to his old home, three hundred and fifty miles from his daughter and current girlfriend, who now also broke up with him.

To make matters worse, his ex-girlfriend, a teacher like him, had in the meantime moved to a small village in the remote West with his older daughter. Now he wouldn't see either of his children much. Bakang was made vice principal. But, looking back, he says it was more important to him that he became a better Motswana by getting to know his country.

On the veranda, Ponatshego Kedikilwe tells me that he used to hear stories like Bakang's a lot when he was minister for education. When he was out visiting schools, teachers would often approach him, and their stories would break his heart, he says. He would reply, with as much empathy as possible, that he felt their pain but was unable to do anything about it. The national welfare outweighed the personal happiness of the individual, he said.

It is an age-old dilemma: Which is more important, the individual or the community? Carol's and Bakang's individual freedom to live where and how they choose, or the well-being of the country as a whole? Are a few months' depression and a father separated from his children a fair price to pay to prevent a state of affairs like that in Nigeria or the Congo?

Ponatshego Kedikilwe can't understand why anyone would choose differently. He asks if in my native Germany we don't deploy our civil servants where they would best serve the national interest? I reply that it would probably kickstart a revolution among civil servants if they were forced to move around the country every five years.

On the other hand, we do have a similar system, albeit on a smaller scale. A friend of mine is a diplomat. And like Carol Ramolotsana and Bakang Nkwe, he is transferred by his ministry, the Foreign Office, to a new location every few years, and not just within his own country, but all over the world. Why is this a reasonable demand for a diplomat but not for a teacher? Soldiers of the armed forces too are redeployed if it is in the national interest—why not tax collectors?

After all, it might be beneficial for a police officer from the rural backwoods of Iowa to swap stations with an officer from Manhattan's Lower East Side for a while. Bakang was paid sixty dollars extra a month while he was working in Nokaneng, to compensate for the inconvenience. A little extra pay might convince a street sweeper from Hawaii to work in the Appalachian mountains for a while, or an administrative civil servant in Yosemite to swap with one from Los Angeles.

The transfer of civil servants was not the only instrument in the contact toolbox of the Botswanan government. They also introduced a compulsory community service; after graduating from high school, each person would spend a year in a different tribal area from their own. Young Batswana were not allowed to work at their local hospital or to go and save turtles in Costa Rica as many Germans did when the civil service system was still in place a few years ago. They couldn't stay nearby or travel too far; it had to be a middle distance, the unfamiliar vicinity. It was a bit like sending a graduate from Chicago to the Colorado Rockies or an eighteen-year-old from Charleston, West Virginia, to the city of Miami.

What's more, Kedikilwe explains, every Motswana is entitled to their own piece of land, free of charge. All they have to do is fill out a form, he says, and the government will assign them a plot. The only catch is that the plot is likely to be in a different tribal area, he adds with a smile. From his porch, he points to the neighboring houses and says that fifty years ago it would have been a given that anyone living in the village was from the Kalanga tribe. Today, his neighbors hail from the four corners of the country.

From an American perspective, the Botswanan edict to integrate seems radical, encroaching on personal liberties. There's no decree, Kedikilwe retorts. No one is forced to become a civil servant. All these programs are mere incentives, he claims; no one is forced to accept the free land. The compulsory community service was abandoned in 1998, partly because the government felt that their goal of integrating society had been achieved. But there are some, Kedikilwe points out, who mourn its loss.

In hindsight, it is astonishing just how successful Botswana's contact strategy has been. When Carol Ramolotsana was transferred to Lentsweletau, she was horrified: "Me, a city girl, a teacher at a village school?" If her grandmother had been in that situation, she might well have said: "Me, a Bangwato, among the Bakwena?"

When I ask a young French teacher which tribe she belongs to, she replies, "I hate that question. My mother is Kgalagadi, my father Kalanga, but that's only my biological father. My parents were both teachers and were transferred, so they separated, and I grew up with a stepfather who belonged to a third tribe. What am I to say in response to that question? If I say I'm Kalanga, then I'm denying my Kgalagadi side. And if I say I'm Kgalagadi, I'm denying my Kalanga side, so I'm just a Motswana." The woman has three children with a man who belongs to another tribe altogether. Over the generations, the tribal identities are slowly dissolving—so much so, in fact, that some have come to demand that the languages and customs of the tribes be taught at school to prevent them from being lost forever.

In nineteen years of teaching, Bakang Nkwe worked at seven different locations all over the country. He had four children with four women, and when I meet him in December 2018, he is single again. He had to give up his softball career too. Who knows? he ponders. If he had been born in another country, maybe he would have become a professional player and had a normal family. At the same time, he admits, he enjoyed getting to know his country. His career had been an adventure, he says, and he is even looking forward a little to the next letter, even though he feels privileged to work in Gaborone at the moment.

Thanks to Thabo, Carol soon began to feel at home at Lentsweletau. She attended the village choir festivals, where goats would be slaughtered for everyone to share. She joined the jury of a local beauty contest. She danced at weddings and cried at funerals. The people she used to detest suddenly seemed nice to her. "In the beginning, I was so angry at my employer that I directed that anger, this hatred, at everything around me, including the village and its people," Carol explains. "Thabo took away that hatred, and suddenly I saw everything in a different light." It's a classic example of the mirror neuron mechanism. When Carol changed, the people around her changed too.

On the outskirts of the village, there was a large field where an old woman grew watermelons. Carol loved watermelons, and she visited the woman so often that the woman started calling her "my daughter," an honorific term in Setswana. One day, she asked Carol if she loved that plot of land. When Carol said yes, the woman gave it to her. Carol started to build a small house on it, but before it was finished, a letter arrived from the ministry. Carol's new assignment was about a hundred and twenty miles farther north, very close to her ailing mother. This time, she had requested the transfer. She could move into the house later, she says, certainly by the time she retires. She would like to spend her retirement at Lentsweletau, she adds, and she wants to be buried there too.

• • •

In his book *Sapiens: A Brief History of Humankind*,[2] the Israeli historian Yuval Noah Harari tells a fascinating story. About a hundred thousand years ago, a group of daring Homo sapiens left their home in Africa and headed for the Middle East. There they encountered a different species of humans, the Neanderthals, and were driven back. Sapiens never stood a chance.

Thirty thousand years later, Homo sapiens made a second attempt. This time, the species prevailed—in fact, it was to be spectacularly successful. In no time at all, sapiens conquered the entire territory of the Neanderthals, not just in the Middle East but throughout Europe too. At the same time, they pressed forward to Asia, the stomping ground of another relative, Homo erectus. Homo sapiens wiped out both species, the Neanderthals and Homo erectus, and emerged as the only surviving human species among many. They became "the humans."

What happened between that first encounter, which Homo sapiens lost, and the second that marked the beginning of their world domination?

In that time, according to Harari, Homo sapiens had developed a skill that no other species—animal or human—had mastered, namely, to talk about things that they couldn't see, touch, hear, or smell.

Many animals were able to communicate to the other individuals in their pack, "Careful! A lion!" he writes. But Homo sapiens learned to communicate ideas like, "The lion is the guardian spirit of our tribe."

Humans conceived fiction, something which Harari considers to be the most important invention in the history of our species. To understand why, we need to have a quick look at our close relatives the chimpanzees. Chimps live in communities where all the animals know each other and understand how they interrelate. While this intimate knowledge holds the group together, it also limits its size. In a group of fifty chimps, there are more than twelve hundred one-to-one relationships, plus countless group constellations. The social structure is already so complex that it can't expand any further without breaking the bands that keep it together and splitting the group in two. It was the same for Homo erectus and the Neanderthals, and also for the archaic Homo sapiens who were driven back by the Neanderthals.

But then, Homo sapiens began telling stories. Spirits were born, and fantastical creatures, and myths and legends developed. It was also the time when, according to Harari, man created God, which opened up unprecedented possibilities for social formations.

Suddenly, humans no longer needed to know each other personally to stick together. They felt a sense of belonging to those who believed in the same stories. "You could never convince a monkey to give you a banana by promising limitless bananas after death in monkey heaven," Harari writes. With humans, this was suddenly possible. "Fiction has enabled us not merely to imagine things, but to do so *collectively.*"

Suddenly, humans were able to live in larger groups. Had the second encounter between Neanderthals and Sapiens been a one-on-one fistfight, it's probably the case that any Neanderthal man would still have defeated every single Sapiens man. But this time it wasn't a fistfight. This time, Sapiens were moving in teams of several hundred. The Neanderthals never stood a chance.

Over the following centuries, humans came together in increasingly large and complex communities. They formed tribes that hunted large territories systematically. They built cities populated by tens of thousands of people. They created empires spanning half the globe—and all those constructs were held together by fictional narratives.

An almighty being created the world in seven days and then sent his son by choosing a virgin to bear him in a stable. Hundreds of millions of people believe in this story. They live on different continents, speak different languages, and yet they form a community.

God asked an earthly being to anoint an emperor entitled to rule over all other people. For centuries, many millions of people believed in that story too, and made history as a result.

A worthless piece of paper printed with the right ink and the correct symbols is transformed, as if by magic, into valuable money. Another story, which seven billion people believe in today.

A chimpanzee would never accept another animal as its leader simply because it had some oil smeared on its forehead. Made to choose between a banana and a hundred-dollar bill, it would always go for the banana.

In contrast to the life of a chimp, our day-to-day human life is governed by groups held together by fictional stories. As citizens we follow laws that were invented by people. They aren't real. The paper they're written on is real, but the actual laws exist only in our imagination. It is the same with the football team we support, which only "came into being" because someone somewhere scribbled their signature on a piece of paper. When we buy a car, we transfer money (a human invention) to, say, Mercedes-Benz, a company (a human invention) created on the basis of corporate law invented by a government (a human invention) whose authority is, yes, you guessed it, a human invention.

All these narratives have one thing in common: If enough people stop believing in them, they immediately lose their significance. They disappear, just as God did for atheists or the emperor for modern times. It also applies to another story, which has become more powerful over the last two hundred years than few others: the nation.

What is the United States? What is Germany? What is France? Nations are like Gods, money, and laws: They only exist in our collective imagination. If we try to put our finger on it, the thing always turns out to be something different: a printed page in an atlas, a river, a group of marching soldiers, or a piece of cloth with stars and stripes.

For more than two centuries, people's belief in the national myth was so powerful that they were prepared to give their lives for it. They sang anthems, saluted flags, and were convinced that they were part of a chosen, unique, glorious, even godly nation, while the others, the Americans, the French, the Germans, the Russians were naturally the spawn of the devil. It was only possible to keep this story going for as long as there was only a very small number of wealthy, educated people, explorers, and free thinkers who could travel. When they visited countries beyond their own borders, they often realized that while the people on the other side may speak a different language and may eat different foods, upon closer inspection they were actually quite similar to the people at home.

But after World War II, people started traveling around the globe en masse, physically by plane and high-speed train, virtually by means of television and the internet. Suddenly, millions of people were looking behind the façade of their national narratives and beginning to call them into question.

I can fly across the Atlantic from Hamburg to New York or visit friends in Paris, and I feel at home in both cities. However, if I go for an hour's drive to the countryside outside Hamburg, it feels like I'm on another planet. I'm not alone in that. Many people no longer feel American, German, or French, but instead consider themselves European, cosmopolitan, part of a liberal urban culture, or some other group that has nothing to do with the borders of the country they're a citizen of.

Every single one of these people has started to believe in a new myth. For each individual, this may seem a good thing, but taken together, for the stability of the Western world, it is a huge problem. Its systems are still nationally oriented, along the lines of the old narrative. Laws don't apply to me and my friends in New York. They apply to me and people who may be as alien to me as Trump supporters are to my American friends. Every four years, we strangers are summoned together at elections. No wonder we can't agree.

The group identities of too many people no longer match the political entities. Too many people have outgrown the idea of nationhood but are forced to engage in politics bound by its constraints. It's as if they try repeatedly, like a toddler, to force the square peg through the round hole and then throw a tantrum when it doesn't work.

In this way, many Western societies are approaching a similar situation to what Botswana and other African nations were faced with in the 1960s: hostile tribes confined together within the same borders. Then, as now, the identities don't match the political structures.

To put it simply, there are two ways to solve the problem. Either the political entities are made to adapt to the group identities, or the identities are made to adapt to the political entities.

The first option would require breaking with the two-hundred-year-old idea of thinking in terms of nations and nation-states, and instead following one of the new narratives. For example, just like Prussians, Saxons, and Bavarians once came together and became Germans, the British, French, and Germans could now grow together as Europeans. The result could be something like the United States of Europe.

The second option would mean that the Americans keep electing representatives every two years, the Germans a new parliament every four years, and the French a new president every five years. At the same time, those societies would have to renationalize and revitalize their strong American, German, and French identities—but without the enmities that in the past led to wars.

In both cases, the respective opponents must be convinced first. Either enough nationalists must begin believing in the new narrative, whatever that may be, or enough anti-nationalists must warm to the idea of a new American, German, and French identity.

Botswana is probably the most successful example of the second option. The Botswanan government shaped a tribal society into a nation by weakening the old, tribal identities with thousands of one-on-one contacts. It then built a new, national group identity by telling its citizens a new story, a narrative so convincing that many started to believe in it. Contact was their most valuable tool in the process.

If applied to the West, this would mean that I fly to New York less often and instead explore the countryside around my hometown of Hamburg. Sean Murphy, the yoga teacher from Brooklyn, might vacation in Idaho instead of Italy, all in the hope that supporters and opponents of refugees, of Donald Trump, of Brexit come together as individuals rather than groups. If not politically, then at least personally, like Laura Messing and her Republican friends.

Of course, contact could also be a means for success with the first option, except that here, the nationalists who voted for Trump, for the AfD, for Brexit would have to meet with other nationals, with French, Dutch, Polish, and Finnish citizens. Over the years, maybe they would develop a European identity too. Why not have a European compulsory community service, or a military service, or a free plot for a house on the other side of the border?

Whoever tells the better story and convinces the most people wins. It's encouraging because it debunks the myth that many people, myself included, have fallen for in the past: the myth that we are condemned to watch from the banks while the river of history inexorably pulls at our world, at our Western democracies, and its freedoms and values. No society, no government is helpless. All they have to do is find a compelling narrative to tell, and a means to share it.

Epilogue

What next? First and foremost, the stories in this book make one thing clear: If we want someone to change their mind, if we want them to shed their racism, their homophobia, their Islamism, or their anarchism, then there is no point in *telling* them that they are wrong, no matter how loudly or how often—we have to *show* them.

No matter how many times Michael Kent may have heard that Black people have humanity too, he didn't believe it until Tiffany Whittier showed up at his house without judging him.

No matter how often Christa and Harald Hermes may have read in the papers that Roma people are normal human beings, they didn't believe it until they had seen it with their own eyes.

No matter how many times Finbarr O'Brien's therapist told him that gay men aren't evil, the mailman needed to meet Chris Lyons before he could truly believe it.

No matter how many times Jamal had seen people on television explaining that Islamists were misled, it took a police officer's smile and Erhan Kilic's matter-of-fact Danish identity to convince him.

And no matter how often Thomas Wahnig's parents told their son to stop beating people up, he wouldn't stop until the neo-Nazi Sven Krüger carried his backpack through the desert.

All of these people needed to see and feel their idea of reality being transformed before their eyes. In other words, the process of shifting their opinions was not so much an active decision but something that happened to them, a passive mechanism triggered by their environment. That means that there is a political lever.

A government intent on fighting hatred and polarization within its society must make it its business to create opportunities for enemies, opponents, and members of the other camp to meet, to set up situations where people can't help but see the other as a human being. But how?

This book is no political guide. It is unlikely that the US government will force its civil servants to relocate every five years. That was a Botswanan solution to a Botswanan problem. At the same time, I can't think why the United States shouldn't introduce the concept of a citizens' assembly. I know I wouldn't be the only one who'd like to see that happen.

The first time I reported about the Irish citizens' assembly, in the German weekly newspaper *Die Zeit* in January 2017, I received many letters from our readers. Dominik Herold, for example, a postgraduate student of political science at the University of Frankfurt, told me that as soon as he'd read my article, he gathered a few friends from his course to organize a citizens' assembly in Frankfurt. Eventually this became the initiative "Mehr als wählen"—"More than Vote"—aimed at setting up citizens' councils at a local level. In the spring of 2019, forty-four Frankfurt residents, selected at random, came together to discuss the future of democracy and to communicate their proposals to the city's mayor. In Berlin, Ilan Siebert and Katharina Liesenberg started a project called "Es geht LOS"—"It's Kicking Off" —with a pun on the German word *Los* for *lottery*. Their aim for 2020 was to organize a citizens' council with one hundred members, chosen at random. One reader told me that, based on my article, he had lodged a complaint with the Federal Constitutional Court to obtain permission for members of a "Random Party" to stand at elections. And finally, inspired by the success of the Irish citizens' assembly, the organization "More Democracy" kickstarted a project called "Bürgerrat Demokratie"—"Citizens' Council Democracy." In cities across Germany, citizens are meeting with their representatives to discuss the future of democracy. In Freiburg, the organization "AllWeDo" was planning to set up a citizens' council to debate a major construction project.

As these examples show, it's not only the state and its agencies that can trigger change. Here, the ideas sprang from among the people themselves, generated by individuals who decided to make a start. In the United States, it was private universities that came up with the idea of allocating dorm rooms at random. In Zurich, at Kalkbreite, it was local citizens who joined together in a housing cooperative. I find this very encouraging; it confirms we *can* do something, even if it is as little as overcoming our fears and having someone from "the other side" over for a pizza, as Laura Messing did in New York.

Of course, the chief responsibility for social cohesion still lies with state authorities. Why shouldn't counterterrorism units look to the Danish police officer Thorleif Link as an example of how to deal with the radical opponents of society—be it Islamists eager to join a terrorist organization or neo-Nazis marching through US cities? Sometimes, the martial pose with an AK-47 or the arm stretched out in a Hitler salute may be nothing but a cover, hiding an approachable person, a searching individual, or a lost soul.

By contrast, any state trying to institutionalize contact that encroaches on the personal freedoms not just of radical opponents of society but of all its citizens is likely to meet with resistance. In the liberal societies of the West, freedom is—thankfully, and rightly so—a precious asset, maybe the most precious asset we have. We've gotten used to the fact that the state largely leaves us alone. In Germany, we no longer have compulsory military nor community service.

It is the nature of the state, however, to impose constraints on its citizens when it considers it necessary for the national well-being. For example, the United States requires its citizens to pay taxes, to send their children to school, and to stop at red traffic lights. They don't complain because they can see it makes sense (most of them, anyway). Why shouldn't it therefore be possible to introduce a new kind of compulsory community service?

It could be one that—depending on the relevant politics and geography—involves young Americans experiencing another state or county for a while, or city kids the country, Westerners the East, or island-dwellers the mountains, and vice versa. There might even be a way to sell this sort of contact program as what it should be: an adventure.

What would our society look like if exchanges between people with different opinions weren't the exception but the rule? Before

I interviewed Sven Krüger, the neo-Nazi, I spoke with Peter Coleman, a social psychologist who runs Columbia University's so-called Difficult Conversations Lab, an initiative that studies whether and how dialogue can succeed as a tool for reducing tension between political opponents. He wants to understand at what point adversaries are able to compromise, and when tensions are likely to escalate. Coleman said that one key to compromise, or at least to common decency in the conversation, was not to look for differences but for common ground. It sounds trivial, but at closer inspection it is revolutionary because it happens so rarely, particularly in public debate. We tend to look for differences, for conflict, or for drama; we journalists certainly do. Coleman advised me to give it a try. Talk to your worst enemy, he said, and don't give up until you've found something in common.

That's how I found myself opposite Sven Krüger. It was almost unbearable to listen to his neo-Nazi language, but then he told me something that had happened in a small town near his. A young Syrian boy had been killed in a traffic accident, and a few days later someone had painted a white swastika on the pavement and written "1:0" next to where it had happened. Krüger said he felt very sorry for the child's family and condemned the offender. He was very emotional, and I felt that he was sincere. When I told him that I was surprised by his reaction, he replied that he didn't understand the current debate about refugees in Germany. Of course we had to take in and shelter refugees from war zones like Syria and Afghanistan while they faced violence in their home countries, he said. I made a mental note of our first commonality.

More commonalities emerged during our conversation: political ones, for example, as we both consider climate change the biggest challenge of our time, and personal ones, as we would both like to spend more time in the South of France. Obviously, those are tiny bridges compared to the canyon that divides us. But Sven Krüger lives on the extreme fringes of society. If I can find common ground with him, it stands to reason that I should be able to do so with most people somewhere on the scale between him and me, and that those commonalities are likely to be greater and of more importance.

I was surprised by Sven Krüger, just as he had been surprised by Thomas Wahnig and Haruendo back in Namibia, just as Michael Kent had been surprised by Tiffany Whittier, just as Harald and Christa Hermes had been surprised by their Roma neighbors. In fact, something that nearly all the people who have had their say in this book have in common is that they were taken by surprise. Had they been asked beforehand whom they would like to have as their parole officer, whom they wanted to move in upstairs, with whom they would like to travel across Namibia, whom they would like to share a table with at the citizens' assembly in Dublin, or whether they would like to stay in Gaborone, they are unlikely to have chosen what life actually held in store for them—to have made the choice that took them by surprise and changed their lives.

Just imagine what would happen if every American talked with every other American, if every European talked with every other European, and if they all looked for common ground as I did when I talked with Sven Krüger. The intersection of all the commonalities that would crop up in those billions of conversations, would it not represent that which we so often try—and fail—to grasp, our shared identity, the cement that holds us all together?

Of course, we then immediately ask ourselves, "How close would that be to what I believe in? Or would it be closer to what I think is profoundly wrong?" But these questions merely reflect our fears and insecurities.

A few days after my article about Sven Krüger was published in *Die Zeit*, several thousand Germans with opposing views met in pairs to discuss a series of issues. My colleagues at the newspaper had had a brilliant idea. Under the subject heading "Germany talks," they had asked our readers seven political yes-or-no questions: Should Germany impose stricter controls at its borders? Should we increase taxes on meat to reduce consumption? Should we ban cars from city centers? Can Muslims and non-Muslims live peacefully together in Germany? And so on.

They then introduced readers to other readers who had given opposite answers and suggested they meet up and discuss the issues. More than eight thousand people accepted the challenge. Analysis by social scientists confirmed that what happened during those conversations is what Gordon Allport would have predicted. Conflicts shrank and sympathies grew. After their meetings, several hundred of the participants had followed up with an email to the editorial team. I read all the messages; the quotes below are taken at random from the first fifteen that landed in my inbox:

"We moved from one topic to the next and could have talked the whole night through."

"Via common ground to more understanding. I got to know some interesting viewpoints of an extraordinary person. A very personal afternoon. To be continued."

"The time spent together allowed us to make friends with the human energy that connects us."

"My dialogue partner informed me that he had no time at the moment."

"We met for about two hours in an ice cream parlor in Paderborn. We had a lively discussion. In some areas, our views weren't quite as different as one might have thought."

"Due to an email outage we were unable to meet."

"Birgit and I agreed that Europe and Germany should continue to impose sanctions against Russia in order to influence the political system there. We are both pro-Europe."

"Young capitalist meets dyed-in-the-wool lefty. There is something very frightening about a conversation with a future lawyer that is marked by the most profound ignorance."

"We explored and discussed our opposing views at length and realized that we have more in common than divides us, all while playing boule. Great initiative, perfect match."

"Exchanging our views on Islam among others was thought-provoking and made me consider the shakiness of my own arguments."

"My dialogue partner and I had a surprisingly harmonious, two-hour-long talk. Despite holding fundamentally different world views (him rather conservative, me more liberal), we quickly realized that regarding the questions in *Die Zeit* on Russia and the refugees, our views weren't that different after all. The more detail we went into, the more commonalities emerged."

"We observed that the pre-selection of the discussion partners [*Die Zeit* readers willing to engage in this project] might lead to the fact that we soon found consensus in many areas."

"We had a very harmonious conversation; our points of view were not always that different."

"We were not able to offer the alleged dissent."

"Having gotten past the personal introductions, we were keen to find out where the other disagreed with us, but lo and behold, there wasn't much divergence."

And so on. Most people were surprised at how quickly they agreed. And many wanted more. Let's just remind ourselves: Many of them had answered all of the questions differently. They had expected to argue and fight, only to be met with agreement and approval instead. There was one email from a reader that I found particularly insightful. He had met with his opponent in Bamberg, a town in Bavaria, and described their meeting as follows:

> I got there before her. I was feeling a bit nervous, as I
> usually do when I meet new people. We had exchanged a
> few emails beforehand and realized quickly that we had
> much, much more in common than divided us. Which was

a disappointment for me. After all, *Die Zeit* had promised that I would finally meet someone who had completely different views from me. I was expecting a [right-wing] monster, or something worse than that. Instead this incredibly kind, warm-hearted, intelligent, and funny woman came huffing and puffing up the hill pushing her bicycle. She looked around for me, waved, parked her bike next to mine, and approached me with her best Westphalian accent. We had a lot to talk about; we see the world with similar eyes. Our issue of dispute, the Russian question, was quickly and pretty unanimously dealt with. We have decided to meet up on a regular basis. We'll see if we will have a proper argument then.

He expected a monster and was met with a woman huffing and puffing up a hill, who rode a bike, like him, and who originated from Westphalia, like him, neither of which he would likely have found out if they hadn't met. From a distance, he probably would have focused on their political differences, which on paper *did* exist. But as soon as he saw her, the differences gave way to empathy.

These emails from our readers, like the stories I collected for this book, remind me of a sentence the political scientist Lilliana Mason once wrote about America. I have come to the conclusion, however, that it applies just as much to other societies: "We act like we disagree more than we actually do."

Maybe we should change that. Maybe we should leave the realm of the binary, of polar opposites, of the yes or no, of good or evil, of us versus them, and accept the in-between. Maybe we should try to ascribe only so many differences to "the other" as they merit. But in order to know what these differences are, we need to get to know each other first.

Notes

1: The Others

1. When I interviewed Rosi and Robert for this book, they asked me not to mention their family name.

2. David P. Colley, "Blood for Dignity: The Erasure of Black Platoons from WWII," HistoryNet, October 20, 2006.

3. George S. Patton, *War as I Knew It* (Boston: Houghton Mifflin, 1947), 160.

4. Matt Schudel, "J. Cameron Wade, World War II veteran and activist for forgotten black soldiers, dies at 87," *The Washington Post*, February 25, 2012.

5. "Opinions About Negro Infantry Platoons in White Companies of 7 Divisions," National Archives Catalog, catalog.archives.gov.

6. Samuel A. Stouffer, *The American Soldier*, vol. I (Princeton, NJ: Princeton University Press, 1949), 592.

7. Original survey questions and answers available at the National Archives Catalog, catalog.archives. gov.

8. Samuel A. Stouffer, *The American Soldier*, vol. II (Princeton, NJ: Princeton University Press, 1949), 570.

9. William van Til and Louis Raths, "The Influence of Social Travel on Relations among High-School Students," *Educational Research Bulletin* 23, no. 3 (1944): 63–68.

10. Gordon W. Allport, *The Nature of Prejudice* (Reading, PA: Reading Publishing Company 1954), xiii.

11. Thomas F. Pettigrew and Linda R. Tropp, "A Meta-Analytic Test of Intergroup Contact Theory," *Journal of Personality and Social Psychology* 90 (2006): 751–83.

12. Matt Motyl et al., "How ideological migration geographically segregates groups," *Journal of Experimental Social Psychology* 51 (2004): 1–14.

13. Arlie Russell Hochschild, *Strangers in Their Own Land* (New York: New Press, 2016), 6.

14. Ibid., xii.

3: The Race

1. "The Perils of Perception," Ipsos, ipsos.com/en/perils.

2. Gapminder Foundation, gapminder.org.

3. Hans Rosling, *Factfulness: Ten Reasons We're Wrong About the World—and Why Things Are Better Than You Think* (New York: Flatiron Books, 2018).

4. The easy solution would obviously be to slow down, to allow more time for research, and to wait a few hours or days before reporting. In reality, of course, this is incredibly difficult to do because of social media, which demands information within minutes of an incident happening; because of the competitive pressure the media exerts on each other; because of detractors who immediately suspect manipulation in any media silence, no matter how brief; and because of obsolete media business models and the assumption that immediacy will help ensure their survival (something we may want to criticize, and with good reason).

5. Paul J. Whalen et al., "Human Amygdala Responsivity to Masked Fearful Eye Whites," *Science* 306 (2004); see also Daniel Kahneman, *Thinking, Fast and Slow* (New York: Farrar, Straus and Giroux, 2011).

6. Kahneman, *Thinking, Fast and Slow*, 301.

7. Ibid.

8. Julia McCoy, "New Outbrain Study Says Negative Headlines Do Better Than Positive," Business 2 Community, March 15, 2014.

9. "Kirchen und religiöse Akteure in deutschen Medien" (Churches and religious actors in German media), MediaTenor, de.mediatenor.com.

10. Ibid.

11. Daniel Kahneman and Amos Tversky, "Availability: A heuristic for judging frequency and probability," *Cognitive Psychology* 5 (1973): 207–32.

12. Daniel Kahneman, *Thinking, Fast and Slow*, 138.

13. Erik Bleich et al., "Most news coverage of Muslims is negative. But not when it's about devotion," *The Washington Post*, October 17, 2018.

4: The Returnees

1. "Jihad against U.S. 'binding,'" CNN, youtube.com/watch?v=8yh-gxb3t1fw.

2. "Costs of War," Watson Institute International & Public Affairs, Brown University, watson.brown.edu.

3. Ibid.

4. According to estimates made by the Center for Strategic and International Studies; see Seth Jones, "The Evolution of the Salafi-Jihadist Threat," Center for Strategic and International Studies, November 20, 2018.

5. "IntelBrief: The Staggering Cost of the Never-Ending 'Global War on Terror,'" The Soufan Center, November 19, 2018.

6. Nicholas Epley, *Mindwise: Why We Misunderstand What Others Think, Believe, Feel, and Want* (New York: Knopf, 2014), 43ff.

7. Giacomo Rizzolatti and Laila Graighero. "The Mirror-Neuron System," *Annual Review of Neuroscience* 27 (2004): 169–92.

8. David Grossman, *On Killing: The Psychological Cost of Learning to Kill in War and Society* (New York: Back Bay Books, 1996).

9. Epley, *Mindwise*, 46.

10. Ibid., 45.

5: The Lottery

1. Survey results (in German) available online; see "Politbarometer Juli II 2015," Forschungsgruppe Wahlen, forschungsgruppe.de.

2. German quote: Aristoteles, *Politik IV*, quoted in Christian Bender and Hans Grassl, "Losverfahren: Ein Beitrag zur Stärkung der Demokratie," *Aus Politik und Zeitgeschichte* (2014): 38–39. English quote: Aristotle, *Politics*, Book IV.

3. Charles de Montesquieu, *The Spirit of the Laws*, trans. Thomas Nugent.

4. Jean-Jacques Rousseau, *The Social Contract*.

5. "Thoughts on Government ante 27 March–April 1776," Papers of John Adams, volume 4, Massachusetts Historical Society, masshist.org.

6. *The Adams-Jefferson Letters: The Complete Correspondence Between Thomas Jefferson and Abigail and John Adams*, ed. Lester J. Cappon (Chapel Hill: University of North Carolina Press for the Institute of Early American History and Culture, Williamsburg, Virginia, 1959), volume 1, chapter 15, document 61.

7. Alexander Hamilton et al., *The Federalist*, ed. Jacob E. Cooke (Middletown, CT: Wesleyan University Press, 1961), volume 1, chapter 4, document 26.

8. Emmanuel-Joseph Sieyès's speech from September 7, 1789; quoted in David Van Reybrouck, *Against Elections: The Case for Democracy* (New York: Seven Stories Press, 2016).

9. David Van Reybrouck, *Against Elections*.

10. This moment is another example of the negativity mechanism created by the mass media as described in chapter 3. In Ireland, child abuse is disproportionately reported by the media. Finbarr's image of the Catholic church is much more influenced by those reports than by the many people of the church who strive to do good deeds for their communities but which aren't reported by the media. The bishop onstage stirs the prejudice that Finbarr O'Brien has cultivated as a consumer of media. At the time, Finbarr did not know whether the bishop speaking onstage had done anything wrong or not or where he stood in the abuse debate.

11. Gordon W. Allport, *The Nature of Prejudice* (Boston: Addison-Wesley, 1954), 273.

12. Sarah E. Gaither and Samuel R. Sommers, "Living with an other-race roommate shapes Whites' behavior in subsequent diverse settings," *Journal of Experimental Social Psychology* 49 (2013): 272–76.

13. Gautam Rao, "Familiarity Does Not Breed Contempt: Generosity, Discrimination, and Diversity in Delhi Schools," *American Economic Review* 109 (2019): 774–809.

6: The Neighbors

1. Jan Goebel and Lukas Hoppe, *Ausmaß und Trends sozialräumlicher Segregation in Deutschland* (Berlin: Bundesministerium für Arbeit und Soziales, 2015).

2. Kalkbreite Cooperative annual report, 2016.

3. Ibid.

7: The Community

1. It was run by the psychologist Muzafer Sherif and has entered the history books as the "Robbers Cave Experiment"; see Muzafer Sherif et al., "Status in experimentally produced groups," *American Journal of Sociology* 60 (1955): 370–79.

2. Henri Tajfel, "Experiments in Intergroup Discrimination," *Scientific American* 223 (1970): 96–102.

3. Albert H. Hastorf and Hadley Cantril, "They Saw a Game: A Case Study," *Journal of Abnormal and Social Psychology* 49 (1954): 129–34.

4. Solomon E. Asch, "Effects of group pressure upon the modification and distortion of judgments," in Harold S. Guetzkow, *Groups, Leadership and Men: Research in Human Relations* (Pittsburgh: Carnegie Press, 1951), 177–90.

5. Lilliana Mason, *Uncivil Agreement: How Politics Became Our Identity* (Chicago: University of Chicago Press, 2018), 12.

6. Pascal Molenberghs and Louis R. Winnifred, "Insights from fMRI Studies into Ingroup Bias," *Frontiers in Psychology* 9 (2018): 18–68.

7. Sinthujaa Sampasivam, "The Effects of Outgroup Threat and Opportunity to Derogate on Salivary Cortisol Levels," *International Journal of Environmental Research and Public Health* 13 (2016): 616.

8. Ian Robertson, "The science behind Isil's savagery," *The Daily Telegraph*, November 17, 2014.

9. Ibid.

10. Juliet Eilperin and Greg Jaffe, "Obama warns against 'a crude sort of nationalism' taking root in the U. S.," *The Washington Post*, November 15, 2016.

11. Arlie Russell Hochschild, *Strangers in Their Own Land* (New York: New Press, 2016).

12. Contact between the two political tribes has become so rare that some sociologists refer the gap between them as an "ethnic difference"; see Amy Chua, *Political Tribes: Group Instinct and the Fate of Nations* (New York: Penguin Press, 2018), 163.

8: The Letters

1. On the Corruption Perception Index issued by Transparency International in 2017, Botswana is ranked thirty-fourth; see "Corruption Perceptions Index 2017," Transparency International, transparency. org.

2. Yuval Noah Harari, *Sapiens: A Brief History of Humankind* (New York: HarperCollins, 2015).

About the Author

BASTIAN BERBNER is a reporter for the German newspaper *Die Zeit*. He has worked in TV and hosts the podcast *180 Grad* ("180 Degrees"), which served as the basis for this book. His work has been featured in *This American Life*, *The Guardian*, and *Reasons to Be Cheerful*, and he has been honored with some of the most prestigious journalism awards in Germany. He lives in Hamburg.

About the Translator

Born in Germany, CAROLIN SOMMER is a freelance translator based in the UK. She has studied applied languages at universities in Germany, France, and the UK. Among her translations are the *New York Times* bestseller *My Grandfather Would Have Shot Me* by Jennifer Teege and Nikola Sellmair and *A Field Guide to Clean Drinking Water* by Joe Vogel.